ENDORSEMENTS

'If ever there was a book needed for right now, this is it. And there is no one more qualified than Chris Brown to write it. I've enjoyed the privilege of knowing Chris for over forty years, and I've had the opportunity to observe him and his lovely wife, Ruth, carry out magnificent work in raising their incredible children.

'Handbook for Dads' will be a lifeline for fathers drowning in all the pressures coming upon them from many sources. It will also profoundly enhance the lives of those already on the road of family life.

Dads receive little encouragement in any media today. This book is a drought-breaker for fatherhood, a rain on a thirsty land.

Thanks, Chris, for living all that you have written in this book and for providing an example of fatherhood in today's world.'

Phil Pringle, OAM.
Founder and Leader, C3 Church Global

'Handbook for Dads is loaded with deep insights on how to walk out the adventure set before us as men, and it's written in a way that you won't want to put it down.

It gives the obligatory forehead slap when needed, and it celebrates the dads who are having a crack (plus it really made *me laugh!). Pastor Chris is an educator, a pastor, an adventurer and a ridiculously fun bloke. This book is just like him.'*

Craig Stephens,
Territorial Envoy, Salvation Army.

"Handbook for Dads' book is fully road tested, and ready to go. Chris and I have been friends for over 50 years, and every word reflects the Chris I know.

There's plenty of great parenting books but what sets this one apart is the concise, memorable 5-minute anecdotes. For those of us who are time poor, or not avid readers, this is a great alternative to ploughing through a hefty tome. This isn't just theory; this is a practical manual for blokes that will entertain and inspire. Let's be better Dads!'

Nick Hauser, PhD
Father and Physicist.

'This book is full of insight, honesty, and hope. Whether you're a new dad, a seasoned father, or a grandfather investing in the next generation, you will find tools here to strengthen your heart and your home. Chris writes on fatherhood not just from theory but from a life well-lived - as a devoted husband, father, grandfather, schoolteacher, and pastor. His wisdom comes with both depth and warmth, offering practical guidance and heartfelt encouragement for every stage of the journey.'

Murray Newman
Senior Pastor, InLife Church and Founder,
Encounter Life Ministries

'I cannot think of anyone more qualified to write this book for dads.

Chris and Ruth have very effectively parented their natural and foster children.

This book is well written and features Chris' down to earth and deeply Christian wisdom.'

Dr Keith Farmer, Principal Emeritus,
Australian College of Ministries.

HANDBOOK FOR DADS

TOP TESTED TIPS TO RAISE GREAT KIDS

CHRISTOPHER BROWN

Ark House Press
arkhousepress.com

Unless otherwise stated, all Scriptures are taken from the New International Translation (Holy Bible. Copyright© 1996, 2004, 2007, 2013 by Tyndale House Foundation. Used by permission of Tyndale House Publishers Inc., Carol Stream, Illinois 60188. All rights reserved.)

Some names and identifying details have been changed to protect the privacy of individuals.

Cataloguing in Publication Data:
Title: Handbook For Dads: Top Tested Tips To Raise Great Kids
ISBN: 978-1-7643052-6-6 (pbk)
Subjects: [FAM020000] FAMILY & RELATIONSHIPS / Parenting / Fatherhood;
[REL012030]   RELIGION / Christian Living / Family & Relationships;
[REL012060] RELIGION / Christian Living / Men's Interests.

Design by initiateagency.com

ACKNOWLEDGEMENTS

Thanks to:

Ruth, my amazing wife, for decades of dedication to our marriage, to kids, and to serving God on our adventure together. I (literally) co have done this without you.

My children: Hudson, Ellena, Luke, Bethany and Keighlan - for l unique selves and bringing your best to a world in need of peo you. I love being your dad. Special thanks to Ellena for your ' occasionally savage) editing of this book. I will make paym ting hours.

My children-in-law: Lara, Caleb, Shelley, Justin and Ch' imagined better partners for all my kids. Thank you my hands.

My father, for modelling some great aspects of l military discipline, encyclopaedic knowledge, ' and to my mother, for your grace, calm, and l

Mac Lindsay, John Pennicook and Phil Prir of faith, fatherhood, leadership, and comr me and many others.

My wonderful Church family: a community of faith, hope and love, and a place we've called home for more than 30 years. It's a profound privilege to do life with you all - thank you for so many cherished memories.

And most of all, to my Lord Jesus, who has blessed me with all the above, and more.

TABLE OF CONTENTS

Becoming a parent is amazing. It's a profound privilege that brings incredible meaning and purpose to life, and can be rich, rewarding and full of joy. It can also be demanding, difficult and at times distressing. As the saying goes, it's the most important job you'll ever do - without any formal training.

Ideally, children are raised with the love and presence of both a mum and a dad. While mums usually bring more natural intuition and nurturing instincts to the table, dads sometimes take a back seat in the parenting journey. But dads; you are vitally important. Our children are looking to us to be leaders, models, providers, counsellors, coaches, and inspirational heroes. We need to commit to the mission of raising our kids. To help us do so, we can gain inspiration as well as practical instruction.

My own journey into fatherhood began back in 1990. I remember the tidal wave of emotion when our first child was born. I felt awe and wonder at this tiny, brand-new life, overwhelming gratitude that my wife, Ruth, had delivered this miracle safely, and the sudden, weighty realisation that *I'm a dad*. I'd always enjoyed being around kids - teaching them at school, playing with nieces and nephews - but this was something else. Now I was responsible for helping this little guy eat, sleep, walk, talk, and grow into a functioning human.

That baby is now a married man with a family of his own. Three more little tackers followed, all now grown, married, making their own way in the world, and most importantly, producing grandchildren for Ruth and me to enjoy. Our "kids" bring us great joy. They're living well, building strong marriages, raising children, forging meaningful careers, maintaining a strong moral compass and walking in a faith of their own to guide them through life.

Since we enjoyed parenting so much, we threw ourselves into foster care, raising 2 brothers for 7 years, with the youngest staying with us for 14 years - right through to adulthood. He too has made us proud, completing his carpentry apprenticeship at the age of just 18 (and 11 months).

Over the years - through reading, observing, listening, trying (and failing) - I've picked up a few insights that can help other dads. I share them here with humility - not as someone who's done it all perfectly, just with lived experience.

While I'm writing primarily to dads, most of what follows applies just as well to mums - and to parenting in general. I tend to picture a typical "nuclear family" of Mum, Dad and 2.4 kids, but these tips are relevant whether you're a single parent, part of a blended family or whatever your tribe looks like.

Speaking of mums, I should mention that I'm married to the best of the best, and that any "success" I've had as a parent is also due to my amazing wife. Ruth is a natural nurturer and parents with incredible creativity, passion and wisdom. Not only is she a fantastic mum, she helped bring out the best in me as a dad - encouraging (and occasionally cajoling) me to find my sweet spot as a father. The tips and tricks in here are all part of our team effort as parents.

I write from a Christian worldview - that's the lens through which I see life and approach parenting. That said, what follows is practical and applicable to anyone. The same goes for my Aussie cultural background which may come through (especially the tips on wrestling crocodiles to toughen kids up), but ultimately the principles should apply to any culture or nationality.

The book consists largely of tips that are quite general, with a rough progression through different ages and stages. It's not a comprehensive guide to every aspect of parenting - there's more detailed, expert input available through other books and resources, but this should help.

So, whether you've just begun changing nappies or you're now having late night chats with teenagers, I trust this book encourages you, equips you and helps you be the dad your kids need.

....

LOVE

Love is energy of life
- Robert Browning

The day after our first born, Hudson, came into the world, I needed to be at work (no paternity leave back in the last century). On the way, I also needed to buy a dummy (that's a pacifier for American readers, *sooska* for the Russians, can't help with any other languages).

As I strode into the chemist (drugstore, *apteka*), I felt six inches taller than the day before. Surely people could tell something had changed - that there was now an aura of maturity around me. As the old saying goes: *"when a child is born, a father is born."* I approached the counter and announced that I needed "to buy a dummy," adding with a note of importance (and perhaps a little too loudly), "it's for my son." I expected heads to turn and acknowledge that here was a man tasked with a great and wondrous responsibility, a man who was now….. A Father! (cue dramatic music). I was on cloud nine.

After work, and with the all-important purchase complete, I headed back to the hospital to visit Ruth and to sit and stare at our baby.

All this to say: parents love their children. But the real challenge is this: does your child really *know* that you love them? Do they feel it? Do they experience it in their everyday life? Do they truly believe it and carry it in their heart?

Back in 1977 Dr Ross Campbell, an American psychiatrist, wrote a book called *How to Really Love Your Child*. It's since sold over a million copies and was a great help to us early on in our parenting journey. His powerful premise was this: while most parents do love their kids, many children don't *feel* loved. He wrote, "Our children have essential needs which only parents can fill"[1]. He pointed out a confronting truth: "Most children doubt that they are genuinely, unconditionally loved."[2] That's a shocking statement, and one that no parent wants to be true of their child.

I suspect that fathers especially need to sit up and take notice here. In general, women tend to be more naturally nurturing and emotionally expressive, while us blokes tend to lag behind in the emotional intelligence department.

So how do we close the gap between the love we feel and the love our kids actually experience? Campbell laid out three key ways:

- Physical touch
- Eye to eye contact
- Focused attention

Simple, and achievable - but it does mean being intentional. As dads, we're often racing through life, dragging the kids along - or worse, leaving them so far behind we forget to look back and see how they're going. I've had plenty of moments over the years when I realized I needed to slow down, remember these little people God entrusted to me, and really zero in on them in a loving way.

Of course, loving isn't always easy, especially when that sweet, sleepy newborn grows up and turns into a boundary-testing toddler or a moody teen. Your kids won't always get it right. They might make some bad choices over the years. But if a child knows deep down that they're loved and accepted unconditionally by their parents, they'll have a solid sense of security and stability that helps them in the long run.

Jentezen Franklin puts it well in his book *Love Like You've Never Been Hurt*: "the very people we love the most will hurt us the most."[3] He shares the heartache he and his wife went through when one of their daughters rebelled as a teenager - she left home, cut off all contact, and even married someone her parents had never met, advising them via a text message. But the beautiful part of the story is how they chose to keep loving her, drawing on God's love and extending it to her without conditions. Over time, that love helped restore their relationship.

So, commit to loving your kids, no matter what. And take a moment to consider: how well do my kids know, feel, and experience my love? What does that look like in the daily rhythm of our family life? A little awareness and a few small changes can make a massive difference.

ENDNOTES

[1]   Ross Campbell, *How to Really Love Your Child* (Colorado Springs: David C. Cook, 1977).
[2]   Campbell, *How to Really Love Your Child*.
[3]   Jentezen Franklin, *Love Like You've Never Been Hurt* (Lake Mary, FL: Charisma House, 2018).

★ PREPPING FOR YOUR PROMOTION ★

Give me six hours to chop down a tree and I will
spend the first four sharpening the axe.
- Abraham Lincoln

Over the years, I've met plenty of successful people: musicians, sports stars, artists, tradies, businesspeople, professionals, even national leaders. But if they've raised children well along the way, that's their greatest achievement - because parenting is the most important job in the world.

Perhaps you've seen the film *A Million Miles Away*, the true story of Jose M. Hernandez. It tracks his remarkable journey from Mexican immigrant farm worker to NASA astronaut. Against all the odds, and after applying *eleven* times, he finally achieved what few people have ever been able to (after more than 60 years of human space flight, there's only ever been 360 NASA astronauts). But the most moving part of the film for me was that, through it all, he stayed committed to his wife and children. His greatest title wasn't "astronaut" - it was "husband and dad". That may not make the headlines, but it's meaningful and powerful.

And yet, for a job that's so crucial, it's incredible that we don't have to apply, train, or pass an exam. No resume, no interview. You just land the role - often without a clue - and hope for the best. That's why so many parents feel overwhelmed and underprepared.

However, you *can* - and *should* - get ready. As adorable as babies are, they're also relentless, needy, demanding, and loud. If you're not prepared to give of yourself - you're going to struggle. I once came across a meme that summed this up perfectly:

"Being a parent is like jumping out of a plane with a bunch of people who don't know how to open their own parachutes. So you fly around doing it for them. Then you hit the ground. But you don't die, you get up and cook dinner."

Becoming a new dad opens up a world of wonder and exhaustion, joy and confusion. But you *can* train for it. Here's a few tips on getting match-fit:

- Observe other parents in action. Watch and learn what to copy (and what to avoid).
- Get some "work experience". Borrow a mate's toddler or cuddle babies. Most parents will happily hand their kid for a quick break (assuming you know them).
- Educate yourself. Read books, attend a pre-natal class, listen to podcasts.
- Join the army and do some serious sleep deprivation training.

Ok, that last one may be too extreme, but *do* expect to be drained and depleted at times.

So, be prepared; to learn, to grow, and to give.

★ BUILD SOMETHING AMAZING ★

All we got is the family unbroke
- John Steinbeck, *The Grapes of Wrath*.

I f you've ever watched *Grand Designs*, or another similar TV show, you'll know the basic setup: someone takes on the bold challenge of designing, building or renovating a home. Then the story unfolds; tweaking the design, overcoming the obstacles, and usually, enjoying the final outcome (though sadly there are a few financial disasters and / or weird designs that you can hardly imagine living in).

Even when everything comes together and the build is complete, it's still just a house. The real story is about the people living in it. That's where the best building takes place. You hope that the same passion, creativity and perseverance will be poured into the family that calls the new house a home.

In many ways, building a family is the ultimate "grand design". You're building much more than a nice physical space. You're creating a relational environment - a place where people belong, where love grows, where values are formed and memories are made. And unlike a house, this project is never completely finished.

Whether you realise it or not, we're all building something. Some are focused on their careers, others on financial goals or fitness. Others are busy creating a wide network of friends, or chasing their dreams. And then there are those just getting through the day, not even noticing what they're building - yet each day, through their thoughts, attitudes, words and actions they're laying the foundation for the life they'll inhabit tomorrow. That's true for all of us.

So why not invest in building the most important thing of all - your family?

It's been said countless times: no one on their deathbed wishes they'd spent more time at the office. But many do wish they'd spent more time with the kids. They regret the relationships they let drift, the conversations they never had, or the memories they never made.

Your greatest legacy won't be the things you built with your hands - it'll be the people you built with your heart. So go and build something grand and amazing.

LEAD

The world, we'd discovered, doesn't love you like your family loves you.
- Louis Zamperini

Long gone are the days when Dad ruled the roost, making all the major decisions while the dutiful wife cooked, cleaned, and carried most of the load with the kids. Thankfully, that version of fatherhood - complete with pipe, slippers, and emotional detachment - has been consigned to history. He might've done his best, but he was often out of touch, sometimes domineering, and occasionally just plain toxic.

So the pendulum has swung. And like pendulums tend to do, it's swung a long way. These days, the model for masculinity served up for young men is often timid, passive, and uncertain. Many blokes are left wondering if there's still a place in society for strong manhood. This is one of the reasons that men's mental health is at an all-time low; they don't feel needed or relevant.

Let me be clear: Men - you are essential. Masculinity doesn't have to be toxic - in fact, it can be terrific. So don't be ashamed of it. Families need fathers who are dependable, determined and decisive. Your presence and leadership matter - now, more than ever.

Children need fathers who will lead them;

- Girls need dads who model what healthy, respectful manhood looks like - so they don't grow up thinking that men are either weak-willed boofheads or complete misogynists. They need attention and affection from the main man in their life, so they don't seek it out in unhealthy places.
- Boys need dads who show them how to be strong and steady without being harsh or selfish - who prove that real masculinity is about strength, leadership, and love.

And it's not just your kids who need you to lead. Your wife does too. Yes, I know, many women are switched on in all kinds of areas, but that doesn't mean they want to carry the whole mental and emotional load of running a household. Some guys work hard all day - on the tools, in the office, or running their own business - and then come home and think they're doing well if they just play with the kids or do the washing up after dinner. That's a good start, but leadership isn't just about helping out - it's about being engaged, involved and intentional. It can mean being on top of things like birthday presents and parties, school admin, meal planning or family holidays.

This stuff isn't less important than your job. It *is* your job. Don't just wait for your wife to assign you a task. Don't be that guy who says, "just tell me what to do." Step up. Make decisions. Suggest a day trip. Plan a date night. Help steer the ship and set the tone.

I love this phrase: "weaponised incompetence" - when someone acts like they're too hopeless to help, so they get out of doing their fair share. You've probably heard (or maybe said) things like: "Oh, I'm terrible at shopping - she's so much better at that stuff." or "I go hard during the day but I'm too shattered after work to do much around the house". Let's just call that what it is: lame excuses for laziness.

Most of us are married to competent, capable women, and we've all got our strengths and weaknesses. Maybe your wife's better at picking school shoes or planning holidays, but that doesn't mean you check out completely and never take the kids shopping or organise an outing. Figure out what each of you is good at, sure - but more importantly, work out how to carry the load together, so Dad isn't stepping back when he should be stepping up.

This will be different for every household. Leaders listen, so have an honest conversation about how this best looks (choose your moment well! for example, not during an argument about who left the wet washing in the machine for 3 days). Set yourself calendar reminders so you actually follow through and don't slip back into autopilot.

Here's a few simple ways you can lead your family this week:

1. Plan a family activity for the weekend. It doesn't need to be fancy. A bushwalk, a trip to the local pool, or a game night. Take the initiative.
2. Check the school app or calendar. Find one thing that needs organising (homework sign off, excursion note, lunch order) and take charge of it - before you're asked.
3. Talk to your kids about something real - ask them how they're *feeling*, not just what happened during the day. Leadership starts with connection.
4. Do one thing that lightens your wife's mental load. This could be doing the grocery shopping, or planning the week's meals, or booking that dentist appointment. Bonus points if you don't announce it loudly expecting a medal.

- Speak life into your family. Tell your wife she's doing an amazing job. Impress on your kids how proud you are of them - be specific. A strong leader builds others up.

Go for it men. Lead on.

FIND YOUR GROOVE

The only journey is the journey within
- Rainer Maria Rilke

There's no single, perfect way to raise children. Every family is different, and so are the children within it, so each of us needs to figure out what works best in our situation.

Firstly, it's worth reflecting on how you were raised, as that will influence the way you go about parenting. It may be attitudes and actions that you're not even aware of, or areas that you intentionally want to model - or avoid.

Then, consider the different approaches people take. Over the years, behavioural scientists have identified four general parenting styles[1]. Of these, only one is widely recognized as both healthy and effective. Understanding each style can help you reflect on your own approach....

1. Authoritarian

This involves strong control and little flexibility. The parent is the boss and everyone knows it. The law is strictly laid down for the children to follow. Obedience is expected, often without much explanation or dialogue. Kids who don't follow the rules are punished, which is often the only form of discipline. Children raised in this environment are often well-behaved, but they may also have low self-esteem, feeling like they need to earn love through performance. Some even swing to the other extreme and rebel when they're older.

2. Uninvolved

Also known as neglectful parenting - this is at the other end of the spectrum. These parents are disengaged from their child's life - they may be around physically, and put food on the table, but they're emotionally distant. They don't make any effort to connect, and have little idea of their kids' friends, how they're doing at school, or what they're going through. Kids in this kind of family tend to raise themselves and often feel isolated and insecure. They may even seek out love in all the wrong places.

3. Permissive

These parents want to be friends with their kids. They're warm and accepting, but they avoid setting and enforcing boundaries. In these households discipline is a bad word. Love and leniency go together, and the child is free to do whatever they want. Though there may be loving bonds in the family, the kids are raised to have little respect for authority. They often struggle to develop healthy work or study habits, and fail to take personal responsibility for their actions.

4. Authoritative

This is the sweet spot - the balanced approach the experts consider the gold standard. Parents are in charge, but they lead with love and wisdom. They set clear expectations and boundaries and maintain them consistently. Discipline is creative and positive, so kids are trained, not just punished. Children raised in this environment develop a healthy respect for authority, while still feeling confident to express themselves, explore the world and pursue their dreams. This has also been called "active" parenting.

Our goal then should be to avoid the first three and move toward the authoritative approach - firm but loving, structured yet responsive and caring. And even within that framework, there's plenty of room to develop your own personal style. This will be shaped by your experiences, your values, your character, your partnership with your wife, and of course, the personalities of your children. Every child is unique, and what works for one may need to be adapted for another. We love our children equally, but we relate to them differently (more on that later).

Parenting also isn't static. It changes over time as we gain wisdom, and learn from both success and failure. Each stage demands different skills and approaches, so keep discovering what being a dad looks like as you progress.

Most importantly, don't try to be someone you're not; some dads are great sportsmen, or musicians, or craftsmen, or intellectual giants - some are (annoyingly) all of these, and more. Avoid the temptation to compare, compete or copy in order to impress your kids or give them a perfect role model to follow. Your kids don't need you to be someone else - they just need you. What they'll remember most is not your talents or achievements, but your presence, your consistency, and your love. Comparison is a trap that only leads to discouragement. There's no prize for being the "best dad" on the block. Just follow the calling to be the best you for your own kids.

So, lean into your strengths, bring your authentic self to the job, and find your own groove.

⚙ ENDNOTES

[1] Terrence Sanvictores and Magda D. Mendez, "Types of Parenting Styles and Their Effects on Children," in *StatPearls* (Treasure Island, FL: StatPearls Publishing, 2022).

TOPPING UP THE TANK

Much of the misbehavior of children is motivated
by the cravings of an empty 'love tank'
- Gary Chapman

We all have emotional tanks that need filling, and children largely depend on their parents to keep theirs topped up with love. When a child's tank runs low, they fail to function well, just like a car running out of petrol. They splutter with angry outbursts, stall into sulky silence, or just break down altogether for no apparent reason. What can look like negative or naughty behaviour is often just a cry for attention.

I learned this early on during my teacher training. One practical assignment involved identifying a disruptive student in the classroom and running an experiment to test the power of positive reinforcement. We were required to ignore the negative behaviour (as much as safely possible) and only give attention when the student behaved appropriately. This was based on the belief that some kids are so desperate for attention they'll do anything to get it, even if it's negative.

The premise was that if we withhold our attention when they act out, and give them attention when they behave well, we'll encourage positive behaviour and see more of it. And it worked - it took some serious self-control to ignore the "naughty" kid as he burned down the classroom, but after the fire brigade came… joking… it wasn't quite that bad, but forty (plus) years later I still remember the results of finding the slightest inkling of positive behaviour to jump on with accolades of approval. Over the weeks this boy really did show improvement and the regular teacher was impressed with the success of the "experiment." Of course, we can't always ignore all bad behaviour, but it shows that rebellious or naughty outbursts might just be a weird way of looking for love.

Kids love-tanks get filled up in all kinds of ways. When ours were little, Ruth and I would gather them up on our lap to read or tell stories and swamp them with cuddles. They also enjoyed a good wrestle and rumble, and being chased by the tickling monster. As they grew up the activities changed but the main concept didn't: spending time together that expresses love and offers focused attention, whether it's backyard cricket and footy, board games or puzzles, drawing, or whatever they're into.

The other great thing about keeping the emotional tank topped up is that it helps your child receive instruction and discipline. Ross Campbell again (just get his book) contends that "Only if the (emotional) tank is kept full, can a child really be happy, reach his potential and respond appropriately to discipline" [1]. It's not just about preventing meltdowns - it's about building trust, fostering respect, and creating a more peaceful home. So, keep the fuel flowing - a full love tank isn't just a nice extra, it's essential fuel for your child's heart.

⚙ ENDNOTES

[1] Ross Campbell, *How to Really Love Your Child* (Colorado Springs: David C. Cook, 1977).

LOVE UNCONDITIONALLY

The only way love can last a lifetime is if it's unconditional.
- Stephen Kendrick

We all know that true, pure love should be unconditional. While this benefits every kind of relationship, it's especially vital in parenting. Sadly, some children grow up believing they'll only earn their parents' love and acceptance by behaving a certain way. But every child needs to know that their Mum and Dad love them - no matter what. Regardless of how they look, what they say, how they act, whether they're delightful or difficult, succeeding or struggling - love should never be conditional.

If you only ever give your child affection, approval or affirmation when certain conditions are met, it can deeply damage their self-esteem and confidence. This shows up in all kinds of ways - pressure to perform academically ("you'd better start getting A's or else"), criticism about appearance ("stop eating, you're getting chubby"), or comparisons with siblings or peers ("why can't you be more like your brother?"). Children on the receiving end of these kinds of messages often feel condemned, insecure, and desperate to perform and prove themselves worthy of their parents' love. That's a recipe for disaster.

Now compare that to a child who, despite their struggles, knows without a doubt they are loved and accepted just as they are. That child grows up on a strong foundation of security and confidence, ready to face whatever the world throws at them. Parental love is like a keel on a ship; whenever the storms of life hit, the child who knows they are loved will avoid being capsized, and will right themselves and navigate their way forward.

Be your child's biggest advocate. That doesn't mean you approve of everything they do - inappropriate behaviour still needs addressing, and you don't neglect your duty to teach them what's right and wrong in life - but it does mean that even when they mess up, you love them in spite of the mess - and they figure out how to clean it up.

Unconditional love also means avoiding favouritism. Every child in the family should receive the same affection, provision, discipline, affirmation and opportunities. Sadly, I've seen some parents openly compare one child unfavourably to another, sharing their frustrations with anyone who will listen. The overlooked child feels unloved, unsupported and will be unlikely to thrive in such a toxic atmosphere. Children need to know they are equally loved and accepted, regardless of their differences.

So, love without any conditions or expectations. Say it often. Show it consistently. Be intentional and fair - even with things like gifts; keeping things even keeps the kids happy, and will save you money (especially when they're older and the presents shift from soccer balls to housing deposits).

THE PERFECT NUMBER OF CHILDREN

*Children are a gift from the Lord; they are a reward from him.
Children born to a young man are like arrows in a warrior's
hands. How joyful is the man whose quiver is full of them!*
- Psalm 127:3-5

Children are amazing, and there's nothing quite like being a parent. Yes, it's challenging. Yes, it will stretch you. But it's also one of life's richest blessings - and you'll be a blessing to these precious lives you're bringing into the world. Don't stress over figuring out the "right" number of kids before you start. Some couples try to plan everything down to the last detail - how many, when, how far apart, and who will be famous for what. But life has a way of surprising us, and the best plan is to stay open and flexible as you go along.

Like many blokes, I could have stopped at two, but I'm so glad Ruth was keen for more, and that I didn't dig my heels in. Together you'll find the right size your family should be. I've known couples who were certain they'd have six children only to call it after two - they found their "quiver" was full enough (see Bible verse above). Others started out thinking they'd have a small family, but the kids just kept on arriving, and they absolutely loved having the big tribe they ended up with.

You'll rarely hear anyone from a big family saying they wished they had fewer siblings. Sure, they might not have had their own bedroom or the latest gadgets, but they'll talk about the wild adventures and memories of fun times with their resident gang. I once heard someone justify stopping at two kids by saying, "Well, you've only got so much love to go around, so I wouldn't want each child to get less". If I wasn't a pastor full of unlimited grace, I'd say something here like, "I've never heard anything so stupid in all my life". Love doesn't get divided in a family - it multiplies. Be assured, you'll have plenty of love to share with every one of your children - you simply get another massive deposit in your heart whenever a new baby comes along.

So don't count kids - cultivate a family. There's no perfect number; have as many as you can and you'll end up with just the right number of arrows in your quiver.

YOU CAN AFFORD TO HAVE KIDS

Nothing is sufficient for the person who finds sufficiency too little.
- Epicurus

Every second headline these days seems to scream "Cost of living crisis!" or "Mortgage Stress!" or "Rental Shortage!". You could be forgiven for thinking the subtext will be "Don't even think about having kids!"

And sadly, that's exactly the message some people take away from these reports. I've read about couples who say they're too uncertain about the economy or too worried about money to bring a child into the world. Others say things like "We'll have to wait until we've paid down the mortgage", or they've read one of those ridiculous articles claiming it costs $1 million to raise a child. No wonder people are scared.

The fact is, if you want children, you'll make it work. You don't need to be rich - just resourceful. You might make some financial adjustments and sacrifices, but it'll be no big deal. I know what I'm talking about: I endured fifteen years without a motorcycle so we could focus on raising a family. Fifteen. Long. Years. I know what you're thinking: that's incredible - thank you. Yes, I grieved and suffered, but the Lord gave me strength until the funds were available to ride again. And the kids were worth it (just).

The idea that you need to wait for everything to be perfect - flush with cash, career sorted, planets aligned - is a trap. There's no magical day when you'll feel fully ready. No angel is going to show up saying "congratulations - your financial position has now qualified you for parenthood."

Of course, there are definite changes when kids arrive. Work-life balance becomes more complex. Finances need to be discussed, and some priorities reshuffled. So, do your best to plan and be prepared; maybe some travel plans are put on hold, or you have to juggle careers, with one person committing to be the main stay-at-home carer. This used to be the mum, but it doesn't have to be - you figure out what works best in your family. Remember: what you gain will always outweigh what you give up.

Research indicates that wealth isn't a true measure of happiness or the basis for a fulfilling family life. A study in Germany found that while parents do report some financial strain, they overwhelmingly rate their overall life satisfaction higher than non-parents.[1]

Other research consistently shows that raising children increases a person's sense of meaning and purpose. Money matters to a degree - but meaning matters more.

Yes, budget. Save money. But don't fall into the trap of over-waiting. You can always buy the dream car or go on that overseas trip later. But some seasons of life don't come back around - and having a family is one of those. If having kids is in your heart, don't let fear or finances stop you. When you have children, you'll find the money, and you'll find incredible blessing as well.

⚙ ENDNOTES

[1] Matthias Pollmann-Schult, "Parenthood and Life Satisfaction: Why Don't Children Make People Happy?" *Journal of Marriage and Family* 76, no. 2 (2014): 319–336.

★ ASK, LOOK, LISTEN AND LEARN ★

Before I got married, I had six theories about raising children;
now, I have six children and no theories.
- John Wilmot

No parent has it all together - and anyone who thinks they do is deluding themselves. As Mark Twain famously quipped, *"It ain't what you don't know that gets you into trouble. It's what you know for sure that just ain't so."* So, we're better off admitting we don't know everything and choosing to learn from others, rather than stumbling along on our own.

Douglas Adams put it well: *"Human beings, who are almost unique in having the ability to learn from the experience of others, are also remarkable for their apparent disinclination to do so."* Don't be that guy. Learn from other people; their wins and their war stories - it'll save you a whole lot of grief.

The key is to stay humble and teachable. Don't be too proud to ask questions or to borrow ideas. Watch how other dads (and mums) do family life, and then shape your own values, routines and convictions around what fits your crew best.

Even your own parents might have some wisdom to offer - yes, even if it's buried inside a "Back in my day" story. You don't have to take everything on board, but sometimes a little old-school perspective can help.

You can also learn from others' mistakes. Growing up, I knew way too many dads who were emotionally distant and treated their kids - and kids' friends - terribly. Some were so cold you'd be lucky to be acknowledged. Others were grumpy grumblers - bringing all the stress of work into the home and constantly finding something to complain about. Unsurprisingly, we never hung around long in those houses.

So when I was preparing for fatherhood, I was determined not to be that kind of dad. Then, one day, before we had kids, I heard a wise dad share two simple habits he'd developed when he got home from work. First, he'd pause for a few moments in the car, to mentally leave his workday behind, so he could give his family his full attention. Second, when he walked in the door, he'd greet his wife and kids warmly, engage with them and ask a few questions about their day. He'd bring love and joy into the home rather than stress and worry from work. He'd do that for just ten minutes - and said it was often enough to fill his kids' "love tanks." He could then crash out somewhere and unwind.

That simple idea stuck with me. I compared that to the old grumps I'd known growing up and thought *that's how to do it*. Simple, achievable, powerful.

Sometimes the best parenting advice comes from moments like that - not necessarily from a book, but just a comment from another dad at the park, or a chat at school pickup, or a laugh shared over a sleep-deprived coffee.

Research backs this up. Studies show that "social learning" - that is, from observing and interacting with others - is one of the most effective ways to improve parenting skills. For example, a systematic analysis by Carl J. Dunst, published in the *International Journal of Health and Psychology*

Research, found that parents who had strong relationships with people that they could learn from experienced:

- Less parenting stress
- A lighter caregiving burden
- Healthier, more positive parenting beliefs and practices[1]

In other words, they did it better by connecting with others and learning from the real-life experts around them.

So, don't try and wing it on your own. Stay open, curious, and willing to grow. The good news is, you *can* learn how to be a great dad.

⚙ ENDNOTES

[1] Carl J. Dunst, "Systematic Review and Meta-Analysis of the Relationships Between Family Social Support and Parenting Stress, Burden, Beliefs and Practices," *International Journal of Health and Psychology Research* 10, no. 3 (2022): 1–32.

SUPPORTING IN THE EARLY WEEKS

I don't know what's more exhausting about parenting:
the getting up early, or acting like you know what you're doing.
- Jim Gaffigan

A newborn usually means the end of solid, uninterrupted sleep - for a while, at least. But if you think you have it tough, consider your wife and what she's just been through - physically, emotionally, hormonally - the full deal. This is the time for you to step up.

In those early weeks, some of the best things you can do as a new dad are:

- **Support your wife**. She's gone through something extraordinary. She needs love, patience, and practical help - more than ever.

- **Get your head in the game**. You're not babysitting - you're parenting. And you're in this together - so figure out (fast) what your role is, and dive into it.
- **Take charge of the household**. Cooking, cleaning, laundry, shopping, rubbish bins - every task you take off her plate makes a difference.
- **Connect and care**. Rocking, cuddling, burping, nappies, baths, walks around the block. Lean into getting to know this new little miracle.
- **Handle logistics**. Appointments, visitors, errands - take the load off your wife so she can focus on rest and recovery. Protect the space. Coordinate visitors so she isn't crowded or overwhelmed, but also isn't left feeling isolated.
- **Clock in for nightshift**. However the feeding is working, share the load as much as you can. Even taking a shift of burping after a midnight feed buys her valuable rest.

I know a new dad whose newborn had to be readmitted to hospital just five days after birth. After a difficult delivery and resulting complications, his wife was totally depleted and really struggling being back in a hospital environment. This dad stepped up. He spoke to the staff and managed to secure a private space for his wife to sleep and recover. She was able to completely check out while he took over the communication with doctors, midwives and nurses, and only woke her when the baby was due for a feed. He protected his wife, advocated for his family, and formed a special bond with his new baby.

Even if (when) you're sleep deprived, do your best to "enjoy the journey". You're setting out on a grand adventure, through uncharted waters. There may be some rough seas and challenging sailing ahead, but you'll be fine.

You don't need to know everything, you just need to be present; physically, emotionally and mentally. Because in those early weeks, your steady presence can be the most powerful support your family receives.

KEEP LIVING

★　　　　　　　　　★

Life is either a daring adventure, or nothing.
- Helen Keller

When children arrive, life certainly changes - but that doesn't mean everything should be put on hold. You can still live a rich, full life - just bring the kids along for the ride.

Sadly, some people assume that having kids means shelving all their career aspirations, travel dreams or social life. They turn their home into a "quiet please - the baby is asleep" zone of silence, where visitors tiptoe around and the once fun-filled atmosphere is now a sterile environment of noise control.

Most of those assumptions are completely unfounded. Yes, babies need care and attention - but they don't need your life to stop. You'll still have money, you can still travel, you can still entertain people in your home - even the noisy ones. Kids learn to sleep through anything if they grow up in a household where life goes on around them.

Whatever you love doing - whether it's hosting friends, camping, working towards a dream, or making a bold life decision - it can still happen with children. When our first two kids were little, we packed up and moved to Russia as missionaries. At the time, Hudson was two, and Ellena was just a month old. We travelled through the USA and UK, taking five flights and a month on the road before arriving. The kids slept in planes, cars, hotel rooms, our arms, and finally a Russian apartment. It wasn't easy, but it was worth it. It proved that if you're called to do something, the kids don't have to hold you back. They can come along and not only survive, but thrive.

Once we settled in, we noticed how shocked the locals were that we took our baby outside - on the Metro, to the playground, or to Church. The Russian tradition was to keep babies tightly swaddled indoors for months, worried about sickness or weather. Without realising it, just by showing up and doing life, we were encouraging others to bring their babies out into the world too - still bundled up, but not boxed in by superstition.

So, here's the point: your child will grow up seeing what your "normal" looks like. If they see you living boldly, joyfully, and with a sense of adventure - then they'll learn that life isn't to be feared or postponed, but something to be embraced.

Parenthood doesn't mean pressing pause, or standing on the sidelines. It means staying on the field, continuing to play the game - with some new team-mates.

TRAIN THEM

★　　　　　　　　　　　　　　　　　　　　　★

Tell it to your children, and let your children tell it to their children,
and their children to the next generation
- Joel 1:3

All kinds of stuff gets passed down through the generations - family recipes, quirky sayings, mannerisms, traditions and values. Some of it we do on purpose, but a lot of it happens without us even realising. That's why we need to be intentional about what we're passing on to our kids. We're not just raising children, we're shaping future adults.

Your influence matters. The truth you've learned, the convictions you hold, the practical life skills you've picked up along the way - these are things worth handing down. Don't just feed and clothe your kids and send them off 'to get an education' - their best education starts in the home. Too many parents today are outsourcing what is really their job; teaching, guiding, training. Dads can be particularly guilty of this when we get consumed by work or too focused on our own hobbies, leaving the most important job of parenting to the wife and others.

Don't be afraid to tell your kids what's right and wrong - you know things that should be passed on. I believe there are three main reasons parents back away from this:

1. They're unsure about their own convictions, especially when those values clash with what's being pushed in the media or broader culture.
2. They don't want to impose their beliefs on their children, because the message they're hearing from society is that kids are "free spirits" who need to "find their own truth".
3. They're afraid of losing connection with their kids, thinking that being the "cool parent" is more important than being an authority figure.

These beliefs (often subliminal) are based on fear and ignorance, assuming that imposing authority or discipline will turn our kids off from having a close connection with us. But as a psychologist said recently on a podcast: "you can be your child's friend when they're young or when they're old, but not both - you have to choose"

The fact is kids are always being influenced. If your voice isn't loud enough, another will be. Whether it's peers, teachers, or influencers on social media, children are constantly soaking up messages about what matters, what's true, and how to live. So don't leave it to someone else - be an influence.

Parenting is a bit like being a sports trainer or coach, who has a position of authority and influence over a team or athlete. I've seen my fair share of these over the years;

I had one rugby coach who was so serious and wound up about winning you'd think we were playing for the world cup every Saturday. He was trying his best, but his influence over the team actually diminished over time, because his goals were unrealistic, and there was little personal connection with the players. He was a bit like those parents who expect their kids to be super high achievers and drive them to excel, sometimes way beyond what the kids are naturally gifted for. So, influencing your kids doesn't mean pushing them, controlling them or yelling at them (or as we did every Saturday, getting in a huddle and swearing loudly about how you're going to crush the opposition).

Compare that to a brilliant rugby coach my son Hudson had; Fred, a local legend where I live, who's taken motley crews of young kids and coached them for years until their teens, when they invariably become a competitive unit capable of winning premierships. With Hudson, this journey began when he was eight years old, and after eight years they won the grand final - and again two years after that. But it wasn't just about winning; Fred made the game fun at the same time. He was able to strike the balance between striving to succeed while still enjoying just having a go. He would encourage the boys when they were down, or had a kid who wasn't firing on all cylinders, but he also called a spade a spade and exerted his influence when it was needed; pointing out what needed to improve and occasionally giving them quite a serve to rev them up and play their best. Hudson went on to play at a high level, including the Australian Army and Combined Defence Forces teams, but he'll tell you that the best coach he's ever played under was Fred. Too many rugby stories? - sorry, but after all, it is The Game They Play in Heaven. Back to parenting…. The point is, Fred's coaching was like a great dad - who encourages his kids, but at the same time speaks up and gives direction - and correction - when they need it.

You won't be the only influence in your kids' lives, and you can't control everything they're exposed to, but you can be a constant guiding light to help them find their way in the world. So don't step back. Step up, and train them.

LOOK AFTER YOURSELF

"Therefore take heed to yourselves and to all the flock,
among which the Holy Spirit has made you overseers"
Acts 20: 28 NKJV

Good parenting is all about being selfless, rather than selfish. But you can't give what you haven't got. If you're running on empty, and struggling to just get through the day, you won't be your best dad-self. So, you need some 'me time' in order to stay fresh, strong and sane.

That doesn't mean disappearing for long solo holidays or locking yourself away in the man-cave for hours on end. But it *does* mean that it's completely valid - in fact essential - to take time for yourself so you stay physically, spiritually and emotionally healthy.

In the same way that couples tag team parenting, it's useful to work out how you can tag team rest and leisure as well. Think carefully about what 'fills your cup' and then have a strategic conversation about how you can make that work for each other. When it comes to scheduling our busy lives (especially when kids are young) it's easy for the social sports team or annual weekend away with friends to fall to the bottom of the list, but prioritising these activities can be a gamechanger in feeling refreshed and energised as parents and as a couple. Taking time out from front-line parenting can even be as simple as popping out for a short errand ("Where can she be? How long does it take to buy eggs?!").

If you've got grandparents nearby, use them! Offload the kids (ideally with some warning) - whether it's just for a date night, or even a weekend away. This is not being a slack parent, it's being wise; simply taking time to rest and reset, ready to head back to the front lines.

Remember that family outings and holidays aren't just for the kids - they're for you too. If Dad is unwinding and having fun, that filters through the whole family so the kids will love it too.

Also, don't expect to be a perfect parent who's on tap all the time. Set realistic expectations for yourself - you can't be everywhere at once or meet every need instantly. Pace yourself, rather than getting exhausted and depleted trying to do too much.

Finally, don't underestimate the power of the little things in life; a hot shower, a chat with a mate, a quick workout or even just a walk. They all help to keep you strong, steady and available to give your best to your kids.

★ THE BEST THINGS IN LIFE AREN'T FREE ★

Life wasn't meant to be easy, my child,
but take courage: it can be delightful!
- George Bernard Shaw

Poor Malcolm Fraser. Back in the 1970s, the Australian Prime Minister was trying to address the rising cost of living that everyday Aussies were facing. He quoted only the first half of that famous George Bernard Shaw quote above; *"life wasn't meant to be easy"*. His political opponents pounced on it, painting him as cold, unsympathetic and out of touch with his fellow countrymen. But he left off the best bit: *"... but take courage: it can be delightful!"*.

Parenting is the perfect example of the full truth of that quote. It's not designed or destined to be anything but hard work, but at the same time it's incredibly rewarding and wonderful. Anything of great value is worth the price you pay for it, and there's nothing more valuable than your children, and the privilege of raising them.

So, when people say, "the best things in life are free" they're only half right. Sure - love, joy, and family don't come with a price tag - but they do come with a cost. Not financial, but personal. Raising kids will cost you time, energy, sleep, and patience (some would say even your sanity). You'll have times when you will feel exhausted, unappreciated, and stretched to your limits.

I heard Kiwi comedian and father Bret McKenzie share on a podcast about just how exhausting parenting can be. After having two kids, he and his wife had a third: "...And then the third one, you are just a wreck. You're just lying down, dragging yourself around, and it's an absolute blur. I remember waking up going, 'I can't wait to go back to bed.'" Despite the exhaustion, he spoke with genuine warmth about how much he loves being a dad, and how the sacrifices are absolutely worth it. For him, that even meant moving his family back to New Zealand from Los Angeles - where he'd won an Academy Award for songwriting. He turned down some very lucrative career opportunities to prioritise family life over fame and fortune.

The good news is: any price you pay to raise a great family is worth it. You're investing in one of the most important jobs in the world. You'll get immense satisfaction from rising to the challenge and sticking with it.

So, take courage and carry on. Parenting wasn't meant to be easy, but it can be delightful.

DISCIPLINE IS NOT A DIRTY WORD

Let parents bequeath to their children not riches,
but the spirit of reverence.
- Plato

Discipline is great. It's an essential part of a good parent's toolkit, and works hand-in-hand with love - not against it. We all know we must love our kids, but not everyone realises that discipline is part of that love. If you really love your child, you'll be brave enough to show them what's right, teach them what appropriate behaviour looks like, and bring in consequences when needed to help them get back on track.

These days, our culture tends to promote the idea that every child is a free spirit who should chart their own course in life, with little or no interference or constraints. Alongside that is the mistaken belief that any kind of discipline crushes their spirit or damages their emotional development. But the truth is, when it's done well, discipline is a positive, healthy and helpful part of raising children. As parenting authors Nicky and Sila Lee put it, "Discipline involves teaching, guiding and training, as well as correcting - with unpleasant consequences if necessary. Putting appropriate boundaries around our child's behaviour lays a good foundation on which character, self-discipline and maturity can be built."[1]

As adults, we all accept the need for rules: drive on one side of the road, don't steal, try not to punch people when they're annoying, etc. Children also need rules and boundaries, and your job as a parent is to set them and ensure they're followed, for the good of your child, your family and society at large.

A child who's never had to listen, submit or obey can become a menace - firstly in the family, and eventually in the wider community. If you haven't noticed this yourself, just ask any schoolteacher for confirmation - they'll tell you that most of the time, the kids who act out at school are those living without healthy boundaries and discipline at home.

Just as the Police aren't the bad guys when they're enforcing the law, parents are doing the right thing when they exert their authority to teach their kids the value of good rules for living. So don't back away from this - it's not a power trip for parents, or about being harsh or controlling - it's about lovingly providing structure and consistency in a calm, considered way.

Consequences will vary depending on your child's age, the situation, and your family culture. For younger kids, a minute for 'time out' can feel like forever (a rough guide is one minute per year of age). For older kids, removing a privilege or screen time might hit the mark more effectively. Corporal punishment can also play a role when it's used wisely and carefully, but this involves a bigger discussion than what we have time for here.

Of course, discipline and behaviour modification isn't all about punishments and negative consequences. Encouraging good behaviour with praise, rewards, or a simple "well done" helps teach kids not just what is wrong, but importantly, what is right. We found rewards charts worked when the kids were little; each child would receive a sticker for good behaviour (doing their chores, demonstrating kindness, not throttling their brother etc.) and then when a certain number was reached they'd be rewarded with a 'special night', which was dinner of their choice, a fancy table setting (with the fine china reserved for the award winner). We made sure each kid got the required number of stars or stickers, even if it took some longer than others (you know who you are).

As important as it is to discipline your child, it's also critical to know when *not* to discipline. Never punish your kids for accidents or for things they didn't know were wrong. Make sure they actually understand the rules before holding them accountable for breaking them. Above all, *you* need to be disciplined; stay in control of your emotions, and never discipline in a moment of anger or frustration. If your child has misbehaved and you have a "situation that needs addressing," count to ten (or fifty), take some deep breaths, or even leave the room for a moment to cool down. Then come back and apply any consequences calmly.

Afterwards, talk it through. Explain why they were disciplined and let them know it's to help them grow. And be sure to remind them that they are absolute champions - the behaviour must be dealt with, but the child still needs to know they are loved, accepted, and valued.

⚙ ENDNOTES

[1] Nicky and Sila Lee, *The Parenting Book* (Alpha International, 2009), 175.

LOVE = LISTENING

Being heard is so close to being loved that for the average person they are almost indistinguishable.
- David Augsburger

Mothers often have a sixth sense for what kind of cry their baby is making. When our newborns cried, I'd generally go into a classic Dad-panic, assuming something terrible was happening. Ruth, meanwhile, would calmly explain that it was just the "I'm hungry" cry, or the "I'm tired" cry, or sometimes the "Mum, why doesn't Dad have a clue?" cry. Thankfully, kids eventually learn to speak in a language even fathers can understand. And once they do, they *love* to express themselves.

It's amazing how detailed and passionate a little kid can be about something that, to adults, seems completely unimportant or uninteresting. But to them, it's gold - and it matters that we listen. When we stop and really hear them, it sends a powerful message; *you're valuable*. But if we're too distracted or dismissive of our kids, they'll feel emotionally shut down. Busy dads are often the worst at this (I speak from experience). Even if you can't give your full attention right at that moment, you can at least say "Mate, I want to hear this - give me five minutes, and then I'm all yours". And then of course make sure you follow through. Don't make them wait till next Tuesday - the moment will have passed (and perhaps some trust with it).

A child rarely begins a sentence with "Dad, I have something deeply important to say". But often what they say really *is* deeply important to them, regardless of how trivial it sounds. How many of us carry sweet memories from childhood of a simple interaction with our parents? The story is often told of Charles Francis Adams, a U.S. ambassador to England in the 1800s, and his young son Brooks. Both kept diaries. One day they went fishing together. The father wrote afterwards, "Went fishing with my son - a day wasted". But Brooks wrote in his diary, "went fishing with my father; the most glorious day of my life". The same day, the same experience, but a very different impact.

You might think, '*what a drongo*', because you'd cherish a day fishing with your son. But the point remains that many dads can overlook the value of just hanging out with their kid because they're so focussed on work or something that seems more important. Kids, meanwhile, totally love spending time with the old man, no matter what you're doing.

So you never know what memories you're building when you pause, listen and give your child your full attention. Sometimes love is just listening.

SAY YES

Freedom is the oxygen of the soul.
- Moshe Dayan

Children look to parents as providers and permission givers. We have the ability to give them things they want and need, and that's a powerful privilege. Kids feel more secure when they know their needs will be met, and they feel more confident when they're allowed to try new things.

We also have the authority to say yes or no to the things they want to do. Obviously, we can't - and shouldn't - say yes to everything, especially if it's unsafe, unreasonable, or crosses boundaries we've already set. But as much as possible, our aim should be to say *yes* rather than *no*. Saying yes helps build our children's confidence. It gives them the freedom to explore, the space to grow, and the sense that their ideas and desires are valid - even if they stretch us in the process.

So instead of jumping to a quick "no" in response to every request / demand / plea / begging-on-the knees moment, ask yourself: "why not?" Sometimes we say no by default, without good reason.

It's also about picking your battles. Save your "no" for when it really matters. Some kids grow up in an environment where they stop asking altogether - because they already know what the answer will be from ol' Denial Dad. That's sad, and you don't want your child to be one of them. It's much

44

healthier when children grow up expecting that their ideas, suggestions and requests will be met with openness and a possible "yes". That encourages them to develop initiative and to be increasingly confident and decisive.

When our children were little, Ruth and I would take it in turns travelling back to Russia (where we had lived as missionaries) for ministry commitments. When Ruth was away, the kids somehow survived under my solo parenting for two or three weeks. One of my battles was dressing them for outings. I remember giving up telling one daughter what she should wear, as she resisted all efforts to find an outfit that was in any way coordinated. A strong willed three-year-old has a distinctive fashion sense that can produce some pretty alarming effects and more than a few chuckles out in public. But for my sanity and for her creative expression I went from "put this on" to "here's two outfits to choose from" to "Ok, whatever - if that's what you want to wear…" and it all worked out - one of many examples where a "yes" was better than a "no".

SAY NO

*Parents who are afraid to put their foot down usually
have children who tread on their toes.*
- Chinese proverb

You know what's best for your children - more than they do. That also means knowing what's *not* good for them, and being strong enough to say no when necessary. It may sound obvious, but some parents shy away from this, afraid that denying their child will somehow crush their spirit. Add to that the modern cultural push to let kids explore the world entirely on their own terms - with minimal boundaries or correction - and you can see how "no" has become unfashionable.

Your child isn't going to thank you for stepping in and setting limits - although if you stick it out their adult self will be grateful - we've done this long enough to enjoy those moments. But while they're little, saying no to too much sugar, too late a bedtime, hours of gaming, or watching things they're not ready for is all part of loving and responsible parenting.

You can usually spot the parents who've established this early on. By the time their kids are four or five, there's usually no major drama when Mum or Dad says, "Alright kids, we're going now" or "time for bed". Compare that to the parents still struggling to exert any kind of authority and pleading: "Kids, for the *fifth* time, can we *please* go? We're really running late". Boundaries established early on lead to smoother family life later.

Of course, some parenting experts advocate avoiding negative language. Rather than a blunt "no", they suggest rephrasing; instead of "no you can't have ice cream", try "we can have ice cream another time". It's a helpful approach - especially with young kids - as it softens the refusal while still reinforcing your authority. The goal is to guide them without crushing them emotionally.

But let's be clear; occasionally a simple, unambiguous "no" is perfectly healthy. It's good for a child to respect authority, even (one could argue, *especially*) when it goes against what they want. That prepares them for the future, where they'll need to deal with all kinds of authority: teachers, bosses, and others in positions of power, who won't always sugar-coat things. Dealing with a simple "no" helps them develop self-control and emotional resilience when things don't go their way.

So be wise. Pick your moments. Sometimes a gentle re-direction is enough. Other times, a firm "no" is exactly what's needed. Either way, your child will be better off knowing that someone loves them enough to set a boundary, and stick to it.

KEEP IT TOGETHER

I am not afraid of storms, for I am learning how to sail my ship
- Louisa May Alcott

et's be honest - your children sometimes drive you up the wall. It's easy to get frustrated, disappointed, or even angry over the endless things kids do: they break things, spill things, and lose things. They disobey you, disregard you, and sometimes completely disillusion you. They'll fight with siblings, deliberately push your buttons, and throw full-scale tantrums - all before breakfast! Even at the best of times, a tired dad might be tempted to cynically think of his kids as sponges, who soak up every ounce of time and energy he has.

And yet - they are precious. They've been entrusted to us, not just to survive childhood, but to be lovingly guided through it. What they need most are parents who will be calm, nurturing and dependable, and who don't lose their cool every five minutes.

Some people are naturally calm under pressure - and then there's the rest of us. Parenting may be difficult, but it's worth all the effort - not only for your kids' sake, but for your own personal growth. It's one of life's great training grounds. Over time, you'll find yourself developing patience, kindness, perseverance, humility, wisdom, and confidence. And if nothing else, it'll definitely boost your prayer life. When the little angels are not acting quite so angelic, turn to God for help and strength. You'll soon be experiencing what the Bible promises in James 4:8: *"draw near to God and He will draw near to you."* Sometimes the most powerful thing you can do as a parent is to pause, breathe, pray - and reset.

And speaking of breathing, did you know that there's scientific support for the benefits of deep breathing - several slow deep breaths, completely filling your lungs, holding it, and then letting them out again? It can lower blood pressure and heart rate, reduce stress and anxiety, help with sleep, and even alleviate symptoms of depression. Wow - simple, but powerful.[1]

Be aware of your energy levels. You can't run on empty. Staying calm is much harder when you're exhausted or overwhelmed. Make time to rest. Tag in your spouse, a grandparent, or a trusted friend - even if it's just for half an hour. You're not failing by asking for help; you're parenting wisely.

Keeping it together doesn't mean pretending everything's perfect. It simply means staying grounded, taking a moment, and learning to breathe through the chaos.

⚙ ENDNOTES

[1] Will Houston, "Your Brain Loves Deep Breathing, Science Explains Why," *Neuroscience News*, 17 May 2025.

BE A GOOD GARDENER

Don't be misled - you cannot mock the justice of God.
You will always harvest what you plant.
- Galatians 6:7 (NLT)

nglish poet Samuel Taylor Coleridge once entertained a visitor who didn't believe in teaching children anything about faith or values. Instead, he thought they should be left to figure out life all by themselves, and choose their path without any parental input. After some conversation, Coleridge invited the man to join him for a stroll through his garden. When they got outside, the visitor was taken aback. The garden was wild - completely overgrown with weeds. The man looked at Coleridge in surprise and said, "This is no garden; this is nothing but weeds!" Coleridge smiled and replied, "Well, I did not wish to infringe upon the liberty of the garden. I was giving it freedom to express itself and choose its own path and production."

You get the point: gardens don't flourish on their own. Anyone with a garden knows how easy it is for weeds to grow. If you don't actively care for the garden - planting, watering, pulling out weeds - it'll still grow something, but it won't be what you want.

The same goes for raising children. If we leave kids to their own devices, they won't grow automatically into fine upstanding trees / citizens. They're like fertile soil. They'll soak up whatever's planted - good or bad. If we don't tend to them, weeds will grow: bad attitudes, unhealthy influences, selfish patterns of behaviour. You don't have to teach a child to be impatient or selfish - that just comes naturally, like weeds in a garden. But the good qualities - kindness, courage, faith, tenacity etc etc - that takes some work. So be the gardener. Attend to the garden under your care: plant good seeds with enriching activities, positive values, your words, and the way you live. Be involved. Be aware.

And don't forget the weeding. That means keeping an eye on things that don't help the character traits you're wanting in your kids. If a friendship is becoming toxic, guide them towards healthier connections. Monitor screens and social media - not with paranoia, but with wisdom. And when poor attitudes or behaviour do pop up, don't ignore them. Lovingly pull those weeds out while they're still small.

A healthy garden doesn't just happen. But if you do the work, you'll see fruit in season, and it'll be worth the effort.

PRAY

Prayer should be the key of the day and the lock of the night.
- George Herbert

As a parent, you're a problem solver, provider, referee, counsellor - and in the case of sibling wars, a peace negotiator with skills that would be helpful in the Middle East. There are lots of hats to wear. And with all that responsibility, it's easy to slip into the mindset that everything rests on your shoulders. After all, you're the grown-up, and the buck stops with you.

But if you're a Christian, you have a superpower (literally) that is often forgotten and neglected: the power of prayer. God invites us to seek Him - to find wisdom, strength and grace for all the decisions we make, and all the challenges we face as dads. Too often though, prayer becomes the last resort when it should be the first option. I've been guilty of this many times myself (and as a pastor, I'm a *professional* Christian). Over the years, I've learned that things go far better when I pray over a situation early on, rather than turning to it only when I've run out of options.

I'm not suggesting you hold up dinner to fast and pray about whether the kids can have ice cream for dessert. But even a quick, silent "Lord, help me here" can open our hearts and minds to solutions we haven't thought of ourselves. It invites His peace and wisdom into our everyday life and parenting challenges.

Prayerful parents are what children need today. If you're not a praying person you're missing out on the greatest parenting resource available.

We should not only pray over our kids, or about problems, we should pray *with* them as well. This not only teaches them how to connect with God themselves, it also models for them humility and awareness of The Lord as our great provider.

JOIN THE JOURNEY OF LEARNING

*The group consisting of mother, father, and child is the
main educational agency of mankind.*
- Martin Luther King Jr.

f Dr King's quote above isn't enough for you, here's one from another great humanitarian, Mahatma Gandhi: *"There is no school equal to a decent home and no teacher equal to a virtuous parent"*.

Learning doesn't begin at school. Even unborn babies are learning, and as soon as they're delivered, the learning accelerates: they recognise voices and faces, begin to reach and hold, learn how to move, make sounds and communicate.

Long before a child enters a classroom, they've already been learning from the world around them. That means parents have a massive role in shaping not just a safe learning environment, but a rich one - a place where curiosity, discovery and wonder are part of daily life.

In the first few years, children are learning everything from movement and play, to language, feeding themselves, using the toilet, getting dressed, and more. Scientists estimate that 90% of a child's brain development happens before the age of five. This means that schoolteachers don't begin with a blank slate - they just continue the journey you've already started at home.

As a parent, you're not expected to be a walking encyclopedia - but you are invited to actively participate in your child's learning adventure. Rather than just hoping your kids "pick things up", be intentional about teaching your children.

So start early: that doesn't mean ensuring your child can balance chemical equations before Kindy, but it does mean helping them learn from the world around them: take them into the garden to observe the insects and trees, explore the rockpools at the beach, draw with them, sing and play music, kick a ball, teach them to catch, and find someone who's patient and knowledgeable enough to take them fishing.

Getting down to your child's level and pace can be a real win-win; it helps you slow down "to smell the roses". One of the best stress-busters for parents is to play with their kids, read a story to them, or take a slow walk around the neighbourhood, "enjoying the journey" (or if you're with a toddler- picking up every stick and rock you see).

"ENJOY EVERY MOMENT"

*Every cliche about kids is true; they grow up so
quickly, you blink and they're gone,
and you have to spend the time with them now. But that's a joy.*
- Liam Neeson

Have you had an older person come up to you and say, "Enjoy them while you can - they grow up so quickly!"? As a young parent I heard that more times than I could count. But now - I'm one of those old guys accosting random strangers in shopping centres with the same unsolicited advice. Ok, that may be an exaggeration, but I have probably said it a few too many times to my own kids who are now raising children themselves.

This is why grandparents are so often smitten with their grandkids. They've seen how fast the years fly by. They know that the tiny little tornado running through the house today will be moving out as an adult before you know it. At that point (and hopefully before) you realise how precious every stage is - even the chaotic ones.

A day at the beach is a great example of the total chaos, and simultaneous joy, of parenting. When our kids were growing up, most Saturdays in summer we would load up our car with buckets and spades, hats, spare hats, spare clothes, spare snacks, bodyboards, and litres of suncream for my fair skin. We're blessed to live near some of the most beautiful beaches in the world and it was a fantastic activity for the whole family; active, social, educational and of course most importantly, free! There were a few fleeting moments of peace between wrangling swimming shirts on and off kids, refereeing sand fights, and taking it in turns to dive in the surf. We'd all return home salty, sandy and completely wiped. It would have been way less effort to stay home and put the TV on, but there is no question that it was well worth it! Some outings like these will be more successful than others, but even when the wheels completely fall off it's helpful to try and find the joy and humour in amongst the carnage.

So even the mad moments are special. They're shaping your kids - and you. One day you'll laugh at the memories (most of them). And when things have settled down, the tears are wiped, the mess is cleaned, and the house is finally quiet - take a minute to look at those little humans you're caring for and raising - what a privilege to enjoy.

GET ON THE SAME PAGE

If everyone is moving forward together, then success takes care of itself.
- Henry Ford

I n any family, it's essential that both parents agree on your shared values, beliefs, and behavioural expectations. Your kids need the security of knowing what the family stands for, where the boundaries are, and that those boundaries don't change depending on the parent.

That means Mum and Dad getting together, and getting on the same page for the standards you want to set as a family: things like bedtimes routines, screen time limits, diet, dress, language, manners and general behaviour. It's no good if one parent enforces the rules and the other casually ignores them. Mixed messages confuse kids, erode respect, and cause unnecessary tension in the home. For example, don't make a "swearing jar" into a family joke where Dad can say what he likes as long as he pays a dollar, while the kids are expected to watch their language. Likewise, don't lie to your neighbour or fudge the truth in front of the kids if you expect them to grow up valuing honesty. Our lifestyle always speaks louder than our words.

Rather than defaulting to old fashioned dynamics like "wait till your father gets home", both parents should take responsibility and back each other up in real time. That means supporting one another in discipline, decisions and direction. Unity between parents brings clarity for children.

It also helps to set goals and create a vision for the family. Talk together about your values - what really matters to you - and then communicate these to your children. When they're very young, you'll just tell them the way it is. As they get older, you can involve them more in conversations about family rules and values. Eventually, invite their input, discuss things together, and allow space for negotiation, while still having the final sign-off as the parents. Good teachers do this in the classroom - I've observed it myself with my daughter Bethany, who in my professional (and unbiased) opinion is an absolutely brilliant educator. She gathers the kids in her classes to decide on the values they want to uphold (with guidance from the teacher). I've then been the beneficiary of these values, as a casual teacher who has taken her class at times; what a blessing it is to walk into an atmosphere of calm and order that's conducive to learning, rather than the chaos that carries on in some classrooms.

Some families organise their vision and values formally, with a family council or meeting, where everyone gets a voice. Others do it more organically around the dinner table. Either way, when kids feel heard and included, they're more likely to take ownership of the family culture and feel a sense of belonging and responsibility.

Remember, you're not just creating a harmonious household with your family - you're building a legacy. As Warren Buffett has said, *"Someone is sitting in the shade today because someone planted a tree a long time ago"*. The choices you make now, the values you stand for, and the unity you model all have ripple effects that will bless your children - and theirs as well.

Getting on the same page starts with the two of you as parents. And for many couples this can be challenging and quite complex. You may come from very different backgrounds - perhaps one of you grew up in a relaxed, permissive household and the other in a strict, authoritarian one. You need to talk through those differences and the expectations that you're both bringing to the parenting table. Then, as your children grow, you need to make space for their personalities and preferences to shape the culture too. There's no point forcing a formal quiet atmosphere onto kids that are naturally expressive and effusive.

So, build a culture - together - that reflects the uniqueness of your family. Listen to each other, and to your kids. Create a home where everyone feels part of the team, and knows where that team is headed.

LOVE IS SPELT T-I-M-E

No matter how busy you are, carve out time to play with your kids.
- Theodore Roosevelt

In today's busy world, people often talk about spending "quality time" with their kids. That's great, but kids don't separate time into quality vs quantity - they just want *you*. So while you might feel that you've ticked the parenting box after reading them a quick bedtime story, your child could be still craving more connection.

Jerry Seinfeld talks about 'Garbage Time': "Everyone talks about quality time - I want garbage time. When it's 11:30 at night and they say, 'Dad do you wanna have cereal?' You're not even talking. And it's nothing. That's everything."

Kids don't always (or ever) slot neatly into our schedules. That means you need to make space for them. Be interruptible. Be available. If life's hectic, then be intentional and plan some time in advance to spend - sorry, *invest* - together. You don't have to overthink it, or plan anything special, particularly when the kids are little. Wrestling on the floor, catching a ball, building with Lego - it's all fun for them, and it all says *I love you*.

When our kids were little and needy, we noticed a recurring dynamic; if we were busy and tried to redirect them - "go and play outside" or "why don't you sit over there and do some drawing?" - they weren't having a bar of it, and wouldn't leave our side. We then found that if we gave them our undivided attention, they'd get into the game or activity, and then carry on happily themselves. Sometimes five minutes was all it took, and then they were off playing, happy as Larry (I've always wanted to meet him - must be a great guy).

It's also crucial to have time where nothing intrudes into your family. No phones, no TV, no emails. Just you, your kids and whatever you're doing together; dinner around the table, a walk to the playground, or simply hanging out. These rhythms tell your kids they matter.

So be present, be in the moment, and just be with your kids. Time is a precious commodity, and one of the best ways to invest it is with your children.

SLOW DOWN

Hurry is the enemy of love. Love means giving someone your full attention.
- Steve Biddulph

This may not apply to everyone, but if you're a task-oriented bloke like me, you probably move through life with one eye on the next thing that needs doing. You like to get things done as quickly and efficiently as possible. You don't even realise how fast you're going until someone says, "What's the rush, mate?".

More than once I've wandered into a shop on a day off, thinking I'm just in cruise mode, only for a staff member to say, "Woah! Here's a man on a mission!". I look behind me to see who they're talking about only to realise it's me. I thought I was browsing and taking it easy, but they're thinking "What a hurried psycho".

Case in point: when the kids were teenagers I stepped out the back door one night and landed squarely on a skateboard. Now, for a calm, slow-moving person, that might not have resulted in much, but for this "man on a mission", the full force of my step sent the skateboard flying - straight into my face. It clocked me right on the mouth, drew blood and gave me a fat lip like a busted-up boxer. The timing couldn't have been worse - the next day Ruth and I flew out to speak at a church in another city for the weekend. I was barely coherent until Sunday night, and though the swelling had subsided, the wound with dark dried blood above my lip gave me a kind of small moustache look, and a rather unfortunate resemblance to a certain infamous 20th Century dictator. Not the best look for a visiting preacher.

So - what's all this got to do with parenting? Simply this: some of us need to *slow down*. Maybe even stop. Take a breath. Savour every moment of life, especially those you have with your kids. Life's not a checklist, and your kids aren't tasks to be ticked off.

We need to slow down enough to really engage with our kids. Especially in those moments when they tell a story that seems to go nowhere and goes on forever. Or when they insist on tying their shoelaces, and every fibre of your being is desperately wanting to take over and get it done in less than 20 minutes. Bite that lip, and let them learn.

So, give them time to finish the sandcastle at the beach. Yes, the tide's coming in, so the sandcastle won't last long, but the memory of your patience will.

SPEND THE MONEY

You have a lifetime to work, but children are only young once.
- Polish Proverb

When you're raising a family, it can help to be fairly frugal. Sometimes you may have to cut down on some non-essential expenditure to make sure the important things are covered. And that's not a bad thing - it teaches you to prioritise. But like anything, it can be taken too far.

To this day, my kids love to talk about how many times they were forced to *share* a soft drink at a restaurant. I laugh it off and say it was character building… but looking back, there were definitely times when I could have - and should have - just coughed up the extra money.

One moment really opened my eyes. Our first four kids were around 6, 8, 10 and 12 at the time, and we were out and about in Sydney when they spotted a ride they wanted to go on; one where you get strapped into a harness and bounce on a trampoline, flipping around safely like gymnasts. I checked the price, quickly multiplied it by four, and just as quickly said no, assuming the fun-factor wouldn't justify the cost. (and anyway, we had a trampoline at home; learn how to somersault the hard way).

Thankfully, I have a wise wife. She looked at me and said something subtle like, "When are we going to say yes? They're growing up so fast". I should say at this point that it wasn't the first time I had said no - in fact I had got into the habit of saying, "not today kids, but another day" to these kinds of rides every time we came across them. So, Ruth's comment was pertinent. And it hit me. The small pain to the wallet was nothing compared to the regret I would've felt later if I'd held my ground as Mr Stingy. So yes it was. The kids had a blast, and I learned a lesson; that my quest to stay under budget had to be balanced against the benefits of paying for our kids to have great experiences.

So sure, be smart with money. Avoid debt. Budget wisely. But also recognise that some things are worth investing in. Part of wise financial management is knowing where to put your money - and putting it towards your kids is investing in your relationship together. So sometimes the best thing you can do is just spend the money - even if it means splashing out on one drink each.

CREATE GREAT MEMORIES

Sometimes you will never know the value of a
moment until it becomes a memory.
- Dr. Seuss

When Ruth and I recently spoke about our best childhood memories, something stood out: nearly all of them came from simple moments with family. Not expensive holidays, or flashy birthday presents, just spending time together - being swung around in circles like an aeroplane, playing backyard cricket, doing puzzles, kicking the footy, or making cubby houses out of blankets and chairs.

Sometimes it's the ordinary stuff that turns out to be extraordinary. Your kids will remember the moments, not the money. The games, the laughs, the late-night chats, the traditions. So, as a dad, lean in. Get involved. Say yes to the mess. Help turn that cardboard box into a spaceship.

At other times, a little more effort is required to create great memories. Planning a campout, dragging yourself to the playground after a long day, or heading off on holidays. It's all worth it. As our kids were growing up, I would always keep an eye out for special exhibitions, events or shows we could 'make a day of' (especially if they were free). To this day our family Whatsapp group is full of links to ideas for special outings we could do together, as much as time and money (and my family's enthusiasm) allow.

Take the lead and look for opportunities to break up the monotony of life with memorable experiences.

There's also great power in traditions. Around our dinner table, we'd go around and ask everyone to share their favourite part of the day. It became a regular habit that helped us all stay grateful. We still do it today with whoever's at our table.

Then there's Easter egg hunts, Christmas traditions, birthdays, BBQ's, marshmallow toasting around the fire pit, board games, sports - so many options. Find out what suits your family, what you all enjoy, and what you can keep returning to. Because one day, your kids will look back. And they'll remember fondly these simple, memory-making moments that drew you closer together.

HOLIDAYS CAN BE AFFORDABLE

If you want your children to turn out well, spend twice as much time with them and half as much money.
- Abigail van Buren

F amily holidays don't have to break the bank. In fact, some of the best memories are made on the simplest trips. When the kids are little, they don't need five-star resorts or overseas adventures - they just want time with you, a bit of fun, and your full attention. Of course, if you have the money to take your whole family to the Maldives, go for it - but for most people, there are more affordable and suitable alternatives.

Try to take your annual leave outside peak school holiday periods, when accommodation is less expensive and places are less crowded. When our kids were in the early primary school years, we even pulled them out for the occasional trip - a few days away from a classroom won't set them back academically, and the experiences you have together can be richly educational.

Again, when the kids are little, overseas travel may not be worth the money and energy spent getting there. There's little point dragging the whole family to another country just to sit by a hotel pool or playground. When we lived in Russia with our first two kids, we used to cross the border into Finland for essential (safe and reliable) services like mail and banking. Once, when they were about one and three, we stretched it further for a short family road trip through Sweden, Norway and Denmark. Even though we were surrounded by so much rich culture - museums, history, art galleries, etc - we joked afterwards and dubbed the trip, "The Tour of Scandinavian Playgrounds", because that's where we spent most of our time. I was glad we hadn't spent a fortune flying from the other side of the world just to see the sights.

We found camping a great option for family holidays. Seasoned camping friends helped us get set up with all the right gear, which lasts for years and is worth the financial outlay. We avoided overnight backpacking, and just went with car-based camping, which can be quite comfortable. The kids (generally) loved getting out into nature, building campfires and cooking outdoors. It also gave them a fresh appreciation for home comforts, like hot showers and electricity.

We also benefitted from returning to the same holiday destination year after year. Familiarity builds tradition, reduces stress, and allows everyone to settle in quickly. You don't feel the need to madly research new attractions in the area, because you already know them. Consistent family rhythms like this builds strong memories.

Another positive about family holidays - however humble - is the fact that the kids are away from their peers for a while. This is great for pre-teens who, on one hand, love hanging out with their friends, but at the same time, benefit from playing with their younger brothers and sisters. The family holiday dynamic gives them permission to just be kids again, instead of feeling any peer pressure to act cool and grown up. We loved observing this; the older ones making sandcastles and enjoying fun games with their younger siblings - things they would have avoided if their mates were watching.

Here's a few more affordable holiday ideas:

- House swapping or staying with friends/family - often free or low-cost.
- A "Staycation" with local adventures - it's amazing how many nearby attractions many people miss: parks / playgrounds / bushwalks / beaches / free local council events / libraries etc
- Use reward points or deals - I have a friend who works the system and takes his family on amazing holidays, all on points.
- Track deals on websites that specialise in holiday packages - or better yet, have a friend or sibling (or AI assistant) who's passionate about this to do the legwork for you.
- Get creative: a week at a caravan park, a borrowed shack, even volunteering as a family at a holiday camp for kids - any break from routine can be refreshing.

The main thing is this: your kids won't remember how much money you spent, but they'll always remember the time you shared together.

"BECAUSE I SAID SO"

A child who is allowed to be disrespectful to their
parents will not have true respect for anyone.
- Billy Graham

These four old-school words - "because I said so" - still have a place in modern parenting. Sure, they've copped a bad rap thanks to lazy or authoritarian dads who used them as a default for everything. But when used wisely, they can be powerful.

Kids often ask "why?" when told what to do. This can be perfectly reasonable, especially if you're announcing some major change like "Hey kids, we're moving to another city and leaving all your friends behind". It's fair to say in that situation they deserve a good explanation, and plenty of comfort and support.

But not every "why?" is an honest and reasonable request for information. Sometimes it's just complaining and pushing back on your authority. And that's when "because I said so" is all the answer they need. As a dad, you'll learn to tell the difference - based on the context, your child's tone, and your gut instinct.

Words are powerful. It's important for a parent's words to be respected, honoured and obeyed. They should carry weight in your children's lives. Teach them that when you speak, they listen. Don't be like some weak-willed parents I've observed who engage in long, ridiculous negotiations just to get their kids to follow a simple command like brushing their teeth. It's time wasting and it teaches the kids they have as much authority as you.

As you can probably guess, my kids learnt to obey early on in their lives. Luke was particularly good at this. I remember wrangling all four kids into the back seat of the car (yep, you could legally strap all four side by side back in the day), when I remembered something I had left inside the house. I said quickly, "nobody move", and ducked back inside. A few minutes later I returned to find Luke, sitting bolt upright, like a statue. Without moving, he said simply "Dad - Hudson moved". The poor kid had taken my words so literally he was barely breathing, and thought his rebellious older brother should be dobbed in for having the audacity to scratch his nose.

But when taught *well*, the general principle of obedience is great. It creates harmony in the home now, and sets your kids up well for the future. One day, they'll have a boss or a leader who gives directions without any explanation or reason, and they'll be ready to manage just fine.

A final qualifier; don't ever let your ego get the better of you, demanding obedience over incidental things that don't matter, and enjoying your position of power like some domestic despot. Think carefully if you really need the kids to obey you on some point - perhaps it's an area where they can decide for themselves, or you negotiate a common agreement. If they're having fun and making a bit of noise, perhaps "Hey keep it down!" isn't the best response (especially if, ironically, you're yelling loudly while giving the command). It can be easy to major on the minors, correcting and fussing over all kinds of things that we should let go. So, "keep your powder dry" for when you really need words of authority to be respected in important areas. Your kids will be better for it.

SELL THE HELICOPTER

If there is no struggle, there is no progress.
- Frederick Douglass

When we first started taking our eldest, Hudson, to the playground, we quickly noticed how many parents were risk averse - even frightened - about their kids on play equipment. In their effort to protect their child, they were actually holding them back from exploring, and even instilling fear into them about trying new things. That's when we first heard and understood the term "helicopter parenting" - where the mum or dad hovers above their child, flying in at the first sign of danger (or dirt), rather than letting the kid explore, fall and figure things out for themselves.

We determined early on that we wanted to raise confident kids, not overly cautious ones. So, we let Hudson have a go - climbing, sliding, hanging. As a result, he built excellent gross motor skills, and just as importantly, he grew in confidence.

Then we moved to Russia, where we discovered the local *Babushkas* (grand-mothers) took protective parenting to a whole new level. They were often the primary carers of their grandkids (and anyone else's for that matter) at the local playground. After literally being hit over and over again by these complete strangers, I finally realised they were reprimanding me for allow-ing a small patch of uncovered skin on my child, usually a gap between his trousers and a jacket. With winter approaching (in St Petersburg winter is always approaching) these sweet but tough old dears considered this an incredibly dangerous practice, and I was therefore a terrible parent (wor-thy of physical punishment). Having mastered the art of dressing my son correctly, we ventured out again to let him play. One day he was climbing a tree, and I could see the Babushkas gathering, ready to stage an interven-tion. I smiled politely and assured them that he was fine, and that, as the saying goes "if he can get up then he can get down". At that exact moment there was a loud thud as Hudson hit the ground and began to cry. I scooped him up and took off, before I was beaten to death.

So yes - my point *wasn't* proven in that instance. But, as a general rule, it's good for kids to take a few risks. Every physical activity has a risk-ver-sus-reward relationship, so in order to enjoy the rewards of outdoor play, kids will be at some risk of injury. And the risks in most playgrounds aren't terribly high these days - cleverly designed equipment and "soft-fall" rubber surfaces are much safer than steel monkey bars on asphalt that people my generation had to put up with. Even when kids fall, they tend to bend and bounce long before they break. I should state at this point, I have little to no medical understanding to back up that statement, but Google confidently informs me that children's bones have more cartilage than adults, meaning they fracture less. I've also got fifty-plus years of motorbike crashes under my belt, and I can say from experience that the ease with which bones break increases with age.

Another parenting approach to avoid is the "bulldozer parent"; they don't hover, they *plough*. These are mums and dads who knock down every obstacle, so their kids never face resistance. They rush in to fix every problem and meet every demand, to make life easier for their precious children. The kids grow up expecting the world to roll out a red carpet for them - and they fall apart when it doesn't. They miss out on the benefits of facing problems themselves and growing as they learn to overcome difficulties. An extreme example of this was in 2019, with the college admissions scandal in the USA. Wealthy parents were caught and convicted of bribery, trying to get their kids a place in a prestigious university. Rather than helping their children prepare for exams or handle the reality that they might not have the smarts for their dream school, they simply bought their way through. That's entitlement at its worst.

So let your children take risks and develop a sense of adventure. Encourage them to find their own limits, solve their own problems and build their own confidence. You might be surprised at what they're capable of, especially if you're not hovering overhead.

BE THEIR NUMBER ONE FAN

"O, that our fathers would applaud our loves,
to seal our happiness with their consents!"
- William Shakespeare, *Two Gentlemen of Verona*, Act 1, Sc. 3

A s a pastor, I've listened to plenty of men (young and old) open up and share feelings of insecurity, low self-worth and brokenness. Time and time again, it traces back to childhood. Often, it's a distant or critical father, or one that just wasn't around. Those wounds don't heal quickly.

That's why our role as dads is so incredibly powerful. We help shape our kids' sense of identity - and encouragement is one of the most important tools we have.

Every human being craves approval and affirmation. When we receive it, we stand a little taller, speak up a little stronger, and step out with a bit more confidence and courage. Kids are no different, and rely on their parents more than anyone else to tell them how they're going - whether it's learning to play sport, trying something new, or being kind to another kid.

Watch any group of children playing weekend sport. Who do they look to when they score a try or kick a goal? Dad, don't get caught scrolling on your phone, because at that very moment, someone's eyes are shooting straight to you, looking for approval. Actually, don't even wait for the goal - sometimes your kid just kicking the ball in the right direction is a win that needs a wild round of applause.

Encouragement builds confidence. You might not think it's a big deal, but when your child does a drawing, finishes a school project, or sees you in the audience at the dance concert... oh no, the dance concerts... the memories are flooding back... the performances that go on long into the evening... the insistence that parents stay to the end... the remarkable similarities of the 50 items... the prayers for the Lord to just take me... sorry, where was I? Ah yes... supporting our kids is essential, and showing that support by showing up is powerful.

And speaking of support, research supports how important a dad's encouragement is. Studies consistently show that children with actively involved, encouraging fathers exhibit higher self-esteem, fewer behavioural or emotional problems, and greater resilience as they grow up.[1]

One of these studies, published in 2023 in the *Journal of Family Psychology*, reported that children whose fathers provide praise, validation, and encouragement demonstrated much stronger self-worth compared to those whose dads were less involved or emotionally distant.[2]

And make sure you don't just encourage your kids for what they *do* but for who they *are*. Performance and results aren't as important as the character and values our kids are developing, such as curiosity, kindness, or determination. When you affirm your child with something like, *"I can see how caring you are to your little sister"* or *"you're brave"* - you're actually building their self-esteem. That's much healthier than, *"not bad coming second - next time try to win."* I remember our son Luke's first game of rugby, at the age of seven. I even remember the score - they were flogged 46-0. But I also remember Luke's enjoyment after they game as he trotted up and asked enthusiastically, "Did we win?". "No son, we did not. But I'm glad you had fun - and that's the main thing". So, clench your teeth Dad, and regardless of the score, always give your kid some encouragement for getting out there, whatever "out there" may be.

When your kids know you're in their corner, they grow up braver, stronger, and more equipped to take on the world. So keep cheering.

⚙ ENDNOTES

[1] The Fathering Project, "Why Fathering is Critical in a Child's Life," 2020.
[2] Quality Care for Children, "A Father's Presence in His Child's Life Can Be Transformative," 2023.

BUILD RESILIENCE

★   ★

Some things go your way, some things don't.
It's who you become in the pursuit of greatness rather than the result itself.
- Tim Tszyu

As our kids grow and explore the world, they'll face all sorts of challenges - fitting in at school, dealing with authority figures, navigating how they feel about their physical appearance, peer pressure, temptation to act out, and all kinds of other stuff on their journey to adulthood.

It's easy to be overwhelmed by the thought of a big, scary world that's going to devour your precious children, so the natural instinct is to insulate them from every bump and bruise. But as the saying goes, "Don't try to *protect* your child from the world - rather *prepare* them for the world". Or put another way, "Prepare the child for the path, not the path for the child".

In Arizona in the U.S., there's a scientific study called *The Biosphere 2 Project*. It's a massive glass dome - a micro-planet - sealed off from normal weather conditions. After a failed attempt at human habitation (they lasted two years, but were starving and running out of oxygen), it became a research site for ecosystems. One of the most surprising discoveries involved trees; initially they grew faster than usual - then collapsed. Why? Because there was no wind. The scientists came to realise that the lack of wind inside the dome caused a deficiency in what they call "stress wood".

This strengthens the trees and helps them position themselves to absorb more sunlight. Without stress wood, trees grow quickly, but they're weak and eventually topple over. In other words, some resistance is essential for long-term strength. The same goes for kids - surviving stressful situations makes them stronger.

The best environment for your kids isn't one of total comfort, with no worries or hassles. In fact, they actually need some disappointments and dramas to help them develop. Children learn resilience and tenacity when they've had to overcome a difficult situation, which then prepares them for the inevitable challenges they'll face further down the track.

Our job as dads isn't to eliminate every problem in our kids' lives. It's to stand alongside them, helping them figure out how to overcome hurdles in life. Of course we'll step in when absolutely necessary, but mostly we're there to equip them - physically, emotionally, mentally and spiritually - to handle whatever comes their way.

When our eldest, Hudson, went off to basic training in the army, he was thrown into the deep end of physical and mental challenges; early starts, demanding exercise drills, relentless marching, and screaming red-faced Corporals. After three weeks, the recruits were allowed one short phone call home - while standing to attention. Hudson reported that some young men had already quit, some were in tears, and a few were even hospitalised with stress. I asked him how he was doing, and he said, "I'm fine, I think you've prepared me to handle tough situations". Immediately I had two very different reactions. First, a moment of pride, thinking, *'I guess I've done quite well as a dad'*. But this was quickly followed by a horrifying thought, *'Oh no, does he mean growing up in our house was easier than this brutal basic training? What kind of a psycho father have I been?!'.* However, Hudson assures me I wasn't that bad - phew.

Of course, not every child is cut out to be a soldier. Some kids are naturally quiet, sensitive and less aggressive than your classic type-A military man. That's totally fine. But they still need to be strong and robust to succeed in life. Too many adults today have developed a "victim-mentality" - and are finding life hard - not because of what happened to them as kids, but because they weren't taught how to handle life's knocks.

And speaking of handling knocks; I've got another rugby story for you. Despite the scoreline of his first match (see previous chapter), Luke loved his footy and enjoyed a few wins as a kid. But then, as a teenager, his age division at the local club barely had enough players to field a team - let alone a competitive one. Which meant they lost. A lot. And when I say a lot, I mean every single game. For years. Not even a try. Scorelines that looked more AFL blowouts (yes that's 100 plus - to nil). Kids left the team, discouraged. But not Luke. He kept showing up, giving his best (and getting plenty of tackling practice). I probably used the term "character building" a million times to encourage him. And it really was: he learned to enjoy the game without having to win - just getting out there, embracing the challenge, and loving the physical clash of competition. And eventually, as a young man, he did taste success; winning a premiership, and even being named regional player of the year - largely thanks to his tenacity- and tackling (all that practice paid off). But the bigger win was this: his habit of simply turning up built resilience that has carried over into other parts of his life.

Here's a few tips to help your kids grow strong, at different ages and stages:

When your toddler stacks it, don't panic.

If they haven't done serious damage, hold back for a moment. You've probably seen it at the local playground - kid takes a tumble, then looks straight at Mum or Dad. If you rush over, they'll burst into tears. But if you stay calm and say, "You're alright", they're more likely to follow your cue, get up, dust themselves off and carry on.

Get them doing chores.

As soon as they're old enough, have them help around the house. You might need to redo the job later, but it teaches them that work is normal, and that a family runs better when everyone's a contributor, not a consumer.

Don't buy them everything.

Let them earn some things they want. I'm not talking about a toddler having to save for three years just to buy a teddy bear, or worse still, paying for their own necessities. But a primary school kid can do a few extra chores to save for that special toy. It teaches appreciation and responsibility. More on this later under "Work is good".

Teach them to survive and thrive at school.

Not every playground disagreement is bullying. Plenty of teachers have told me that parents are increasingly dramatising the problems their kids face, when in fact it's just a normal part of growing up. When your child comes home upset, listen, support them and talk it through - but maybe the best response is, "Yes, that's a problem. But you can deal with it", rather than firing off an email demanding a meeting with the principal. If something is serious, sure, we step in. But as much as possible help your kids work through the minor stuff - it builds problem-solving abilities and emotional strength.

Your kids are precious - but we don't want to be too precious in how we raise them. Life is tough sometimes. Helping our kids face that - rather than sheltering them from it - will set them up to win.

BE A SUPERMODEL

Children have never been very good at listening to their elders,
but they have never failed to imitate them.
- James Baldwin

You're their greatest role model - at least for a while.

Children learn from what we *do* more than what we *say*. Years ago, I was working in the garden with two of my boys "helping" me. At one point, I spat on the lawn (charming I know, but at least after many years of training Ruth stopped me doing it inside). I saw out of the corner of my eye both boys copying me - first one, then the other - spitting on the ground just like I had.

Fast forward a generation: a couple of years ago I saw my grandson watching his dad wax his surfboard. Immediately, the three-year-old started rubbing his hand on his bodyboard just like Dad - no idea what he was doing, but his brain was saying, "If Dad's doing it, it must be good".

No matter how much we lecture or explain, kids will copy what they see us doing. One expert said, "We teach what we *know,* but we reproduce what we *are.*" Of course, as they get older, they'll choose their own path, and even learn what *not* to do from us, but when they're little they just assume our actions are the blueprint for how to behave.

Therefore, take that responsibility seriously - not as a burden, but as a privilege. Use your words, your habits, and your everyday life to give your kids a solid model to follow. And for those of you who have daughters, consider the old adage, "be the man you want your daughter to marry".

Bottom line: they're always watching. So give them something worth following.

SORTING OUT SIBLINGS

Having one child makes you a parent. Having two, you are a referee.
- Sir David Frost

Siblings can be one of the greatest gifts your kids will ever receive. Built-in mates, constant companionship, lessons in sharing, and a lifelong crash course in how to get along with others. Of course, that last part doesn't always come naturally.

Brothers and sisters will inevitably clash. But this is no cause for alarm - it's just a normal part of the training ground of family life, growing and learning about relationships. The moment a new baby arrives, the older child learns that they're no longer the centre of the universe; they have to share their toys, space, and - most significantly - their parents' attention.

As your kids grow, sibling tension will ebb and flow, depending on personalities, moods, interests, and circumstances. But you don't need to swoop in and fix every little skirmish. Your job is just to keep things fair and safe - not injury-free necessarily, just without permanent damage. I think back to my childhood and pity my mother who tried to break up some pretty physical fights between my brother and myself - we get on great now, but we sure had our moments.

Parenting author Penny Palmano offers some solid advice in her book *Yes, Please, Whatever*: "Always try and encourage your children to sort out their problems, otherwise parents become judge and jury over their disagreements. In a few years they won't have you to do their negotiating and compromising for them, so it's best to get in as much practice as possible."[1]

That's spot on. Learning how to resolve conflicts, apologise, and forgive are essential life skills for adults - and it all starts in the home. Don't rob your kids of the chance to learn those things just because the bickering wears you down - let them figure things out as much as possible.

Also, regularly remind your kids that siblings are special. As an uncle of mine used to say, *"Friends come and go but you always have family."* In your tribe, teach your kids to stick together, especially in the tough times - like dealing with schoolyard teasing, cliques amongst friends, and playground politics. They need to know their brother or sister has their back, no matter what happens.

That kind of loyalty doesn't happen automatically - it's modelled, encouraged, and celebrated in the home. Occasionally, you see the fruit of this on the world stage. Take the Lawrence brothers - Hunter and Jett - two young Aussie legends currently dominating the international motocross scene. They're constantly battling for first and second place, and yet in every post-race interview, whoever finishes second looks genuinely happy for his brother. Insiders say this is the real deal, and it stems from a "family first" culture, cultivated by their parents, who sold up and moved the family to the USA to support the boys' dreams and careers.

Likewise, Marc and Alex Marquez; as I write this, they're 1 and 2 in the standings of the Moto GP World Championship (yes more motorcycling, I make no apology). They maintain a close relationship despite the high-stakes rivalry, and behind-the-scenes documentaries reveal just how strong the family bond is.

Tragically, most of us aren't raising world champion motorcycle racers, but we can still see our kids succeed in their chosen fields, and even if they compete in the same space - academically, the arts, or on the sporting field - it can be a healthy, happy rivalry if it's grounded in mutual respect and loyalty. And of course, that kind of culture starts with us. Don't stress if their connection is challenging or complicated - these are very dynamic relationships that will grow just as they do, and with your guidance, you can help them foster something special.

⚙ ENDNOTES

[1]   Penny Palmano, *Yes, Please, Whatever!* (Harper Thorsons, 2005), p. 227.

THEY'RE ALL DIFFERENT

To wish you were someone else is to waste the person you are.
- Sven-Göran Eriksson

One of the best things you can do as a dad is to know your kids well - not just in general, but each one individually. Learn to understand their unique personalities and adapt your parenting to suit. A "one-size-fits-all" approach doesn't quite cut it.

For example, we found that all our kids needed different approaches when it came to discipline. A couple of them responded well to gentle correction - a raised eyebrow and a quiet word was usually enough. Another one or two, however, needed a firmer hand to pull them into line when they veered off track. Same home, same parents, just different internal kid-wiring.

We also discovered that each had a different "love language" - that is, the way they experienced and communicated love. Gary Chapman's book on *The 5 Love Languages* is helpful here, identifying the general categories as: words of affirmation, acts of service, gifts, quality time, and physical touch.[1] Some kids crave cuddles or rumbles on the floor. Others come alive with words of encouragement or quality time. Another just wants to kick the footy with dad or hang out doing something practical.

Children also express their wants and needs differently. In our family, Hudson earned the nickname "The Negotiator" because he always knew what he wanted and had no hesitation relentlessly putting his case forward - whether it was something to buy or a weekend plan for the whole family. Meanwhile, Luke was much more cruisy; when Ruth asked him what he wanted for his birthday one year, he famously replied, *"Hmm, nothing really, I have everything I need."*

Developmental psychologists back this up too. Dr. David Keirsey, who studied temperament theory, said that understanding your child's personality can help you avoid unnecessary conflict and strengthen your bond.[2] Similarly, Dr. Ross Greene, author of *The Explosive Child*, says *"Kids do well if they can"* - meaning that challenging behaviour is often a sign of lagging skills or unmet needs, not wilful disobedience.[3] The wise parent figures out what's going on underneath and adapts accordingly.

Each child is a one-off. Our job isn't to mold them into the same shape but to help them become the best version of who they already are. Get curious about what makes them tick - their strengths, quirks, fears, and dreams. Then parent that child.

⚙ ENDNOTES

[1] Gary Chapman, *The Five Love Languages* (Northfield Publishing, 1992).
[2] David Keirsey, *Please Understand Me: Character and Temperament Types* (Prometheus Nemesis Books, 1978).
[3] Ross Greene, *The Explosive Child* (Harper Collins, 1998).

CULTIVATE COMMUNITY

The wider the circle of those who love a child,
the more secure and confident that child will be.
- Sally Clarkson

You don't have to do this on your own. Whether you're a couple - or especially if you're a single parent - there's a wider community of support that can help you raise your kids.

One of the best resources - often hiding in plain sight - is your extended family. Grandparents, aunties, uncles, cousins - they can all play a valuable role in shaping well-rounded children. Sometimes they reinforce the values you're already trying to instil, and other times it gives your kids exposure to a completely different worldview. Even then, it can be a great platform for discussion and exploration ("yes kids, we love Uncle Chicka and we admire how he's such a hard worker on the farm - but the smoking and swearing aren't exactly what we're aiming for in this family").

Grandparents in particular can be especially significant. They often bring a steady (and hopefully patient) presence, along with the time and life experience to pass on valuable wisdom and practical skills. At our place now, when the grandkids come over, they love to cook with Ruth, and hang out at my desk drawing and colouring in pictures, while I "work" (read: stare at the same sentence over and over until I give up and join them).

One of my grandfathers taught me two things in particular; toughness and generosity. As a young teenager I worked every Saturday in the plant nursery he had started years earlier. Business was always booming, while the two nearby nurseries struggled. His secret; simply look after the customers with a good product at a good price. Though his nature was classic old timer gruffness, he was actually kind, caring and generous. More than once, I had people return a plant that had died (usually a notoriously hard to grow Maiden-Hair fern), only to find that they simply hadn't watered it. But before I could point out that the deceased plant was entirely their fault, he'd shuffle past and mutter "just give 'em another one". The cost of a replacement plant was worth far less than the goodwill that was generated. He never had discounts, sales or any marketing whatsoever - but Saturdays when I worked (and in fact every day) were flat out - largely because of this kind of generosity. This attitude extended to his staff, who were paid above award wages, and bonuses on particularly hot or busy days.

As I mentioned he was a tough old bloke, having gone through 2 world wars, the depression and building up his business from scratch. At the end of each day, he'd get the takings (thousands of dollars, all in cash back in the '70s), stuff it in a bag and take it home with him in the car. My father and others had asked him to use an armoured security service or at least a safe, but my grandad thought better of it. Sure enough, someone had figured out that this old man was carrying a load of cash and when he arrived home one night he was beaten up and robbed.

We all thought *'at least now he'll use an armoured truck to manage the money'* - but no - he simply bought himself a shotgun. So, when the thief inevitably came at him again one night, he was prepared. I should mention that this was in the middle of suburban Sydney. Shots rang out, and neighbours called the police, who attended the scene to find a feisty old Mr Brown holding his shotgun and wondering if (probably hoping that) he had hit the robber as he ran away. The police asked him to promise he wouldn't do such a thing again, and I can't repeat his actual words here, but let's just say he used some colourful language to say he was quite prepared to defend himself at any point in the future.

Of course, the thief never returned, and my grandad carried on with his shotgun-carrying money management system. So, you never know what your kids will learn from relatives. Even if the moral lesson from that incident is a little murky (self-defence is good / shooting at people maybe not so good?), at least it was a good story to tell my mates at school.

Of course, not everyone has extended family living nearby to entertain the kids in such a manner - or to help out with babysitting, advice or some other kind of support. But even then, the point is, parenting doesn't need to be a solo endeavour. As the saying goes *"it takes a village to raise a child"*. So, find places where your kids can benefit from those connections. For us, Church has always been that ultimate place of community, and it's wonderful to see individuals and families of all shapes and sizes (especially expats without relatives nearby), enjoy that all-important support and connection.

Where else can you find that sense of community? Take some initiative and put yourself out there - join a club, or suggest to another dad a playground meet up or a BBQ night. Remember, you can't do it all - and you don't have to. Find your village.

TACKLE THE GREAT OUTDOORS

The richness I achieve comes from nature, the source of my inspiration.
- Claude Monet

When our kids were little, we lived in a house where the trampoline sat right underneath a window at the end of the living room. The kids would open the window, run across the room and launch themselves straight out into the air. It gave visitors quite a fright - all they saw was a child disappearing out the window - until they realized there was a trampoline waiting below. (this was one of the old-school ones without the safety netting, so yes, they occasionally bounced straight off onto the lawn, but that's part of the fun.)

Taking some risks is good for kids. And it's actually safer to jump around in the backyard than bounce off hard surfaces inside the house. There's a whole world of adventure waiting outside - whether it's in the backyard, a local playground, or further afield.

Back in the early 1980's I taught primary school in inner-city Sydney. One day, we took our Year 5 and 6 kids on an excursion out of the city for a bushwalk. Many of them had never left the city before - their only "nature" experience was the odd patch of grass or city park. These were street-smart kids, too cool for school, and not impressed by much, especially being dragged out on a bus trip.

But I'll never forget what happened when the bus doors opened. They bolted into the bush, laughing and screaming, completely overwhelmed by the space and freedom. These tough city kids lost all their cool vibes as they giggled and yelled and ran up and down the bush tracks. That memory has stuck with me for decades. It illustrates just how much kids crave connection with the natural world - even if they don't know it yet.

So, take your kids out there - to the bush, the beach, the local creek - wherever they can explore, climb trees, throw rocks, build cubbies and get their hands dirty. As they get older, you can let them venture out on their own or with friends. Our son Luke and his mates went through a phase where they built treehouses on any spare patch of bushland they could find. I may have lost a few hammers and a saw or two, but it was worth it to see them totally absorbed in creative, healthy outdoor adventures.

When my kids got too comfortable indoors, and wanted to just lie around and watch tv, they'd hear my oft-spoken rhetorical question, "Is the sun shining?" - which was dad-code for, "get outside, get creative, and get some fresh air and exercise". Sadly, some kids are bludging inside their homes for way too long. We've lived in the same house for over 20 years, in a neighbourhood full of young families. But over time, I've seen fewer kids on their bikes, or riding skateboards, or kicking a footy at the local park. Instead, many are glued to a screen just riding a virtual bike in cyberspace. Of course, screens themselves aren't the problem. We let our kids watch TV, play computer games, and chill out - just in moderation (more on that later under "Screen Policing").

The benefits of outdoor activities are massive:

- Exercise boosts fitness, builds muscles, and releases endorphins like dopamine; your brain's natural "happy drug". You actually get a mood lift from exercise - something a lot of kids (and adults) miss out on.

- Coordination develops through physical play - kicking footballs, throwing and catching, climbing a tree, skipping, jumping and generally running around.
- Learning about the world increases when kids are given freedom to explore. As Albert Einstein said: *"Play is the highest form of research."*

So send 'em outside - nature's waiting.

APOLOGISE

He who is sorry for having sinned is almost innocent.
- Seneca

Sometimes you're going to drop the ball; maybe you'll forget a promise, lose your temper, or fall short in some other way. As your children grow up, it will slowly dawn on them that you're not perfect, and that you'll occasionally do the wrong thing by them. That's not a problem

- in fact, it's an opportunity. In those moments, one of the most powerful things you can do is say sorry. Of course, apologising to your kids can be surprisingly tough - especially for men (so I am told). Maybe it feels like a dent in your authority, or an attack on your position as parent. But it's actually a sign of strength, rather than weakness.

When you admit fault, your children don't lose respect for you - they gain it. They see that you're honest and humble, and that you value the relationship enough to make things right. You're not just the boss; you're a human being capable of making mistakes, and at the same time, capable of leading with integrity.

One of the benefits for kids when you apologise is that you're showing them what real remorse, repentance, and restoration looks like. You're modelling something deeply valuable.

If you never say sorry, but constantly expect your kids to apologise on cue, you risk teaching them to be insincere. A forced apology isn't the goal. You want them to grow into people who can genuinely recognise when they've hurt someone and want to make it right. So rather than barking *"Say sorry now!"*, try guiding more gently: *"See how your sister is upset you took her toy? What could you do to help make things right?"* It's about building empathy and letting the apology come from the heart, not just from fear of punishment.

Daniel Siegel and Tina Payne Bryson write in their book *The Whole-Brain Child*, "Parents who admit their mistakes teach children that it's okay to be imperfect—and that what matters most is how we respond when we've done wrong."[1]

So, if - that is - when - you miss it and mess up, own it, apologise, and see your children grow up with the ability to do the same.

⚙ ENDNOTES

[1] Daniel J. Siegel and Tina Payne Bryson, *The Whole-Brain Child: 12 Revolutionary Strategies to Nurture Your Child's Developing Mind* (Bantam Publishers, 2012).

BELIEVE FOR HEALTH AND HEALING

You have a right to healing as well as forgiveness when you believe.
- T.L. Osborn

If you believe in God, then believe in His ability - and willingness - to heal. The Bible is full of promises about healing. Jesus Himself said that one of the signs of those who believe in Him is that *"they will lay hands on the sick and they will recover"* (Mark 16:18). So don't hesitate to pray boldly for your kids to be healthy and whole.

Of course, we're grateful for modern medicine and all the brilliant advances it brings. But when the doctors don't have all the answers, we have a higher authority to turn to. Sometimes, prayer and faith in God's healing power is the only option left.

We experienced this firsthand while living in Russia in the early 1990's, where medical care was… let's just say, sub-optimal. Our eldest, Hudson, about three at the time, came down with a severe fever and illness of some kind that left him weak and lifeless. Local doctors had no answers. We prayed, but also decided to make an emergency trip to Finland the next morning - a three-hour drive that we could make because our car had international number plates, required by Russian authorities to leave the country.

But when we woke up, we found the plates had been stolen. Without them, we couldn't cross the border. Finland - and its wonderfully efficient health care system - was no longer an option. All we had left was prayer - and, as it turned out, that was all we needed. We pressed into God, stood on His Word, and fought through for our son to be healed. And we came out stronger in our faith, more confident in healing prayer, and ready for future battles.

Around that same time, a very different health scare showed up - involving watermelons. They were suddenly being sold off the back of trucks arriving from the south. This was a rare treat, since fresh fruit and vegetables were rarely available in our northern city of St Petersburg. We had been feeding our kids watermelon every day for weeks - until Ruth got a phone call from a friend in the U.S. Embassy.

"Have you seen those watermelons for sale?" they asked. "Yes," Ruth replied. "Well, don't eat them! They're radioactive!". It turned out that the melons had been grown in the Chernobyl region, where the soil was still contaminated after the nuclear disaster six years earlier. The Americans had tested them and found high levels of radiation.

Ruth looked across the room at our two children… who were - at that very moment - munching away on their latest watermelon. That situation called for some very focussed prayer. And once again, God's word was available. The same verse from Mark 16 I quoted earlier contains another power-ful - and unusual - promise: *"If they drink anything poisonous, it won't hurt them"*. Until then, we'd never had a reason to claim that part of the verse (I mean, who goes around drinking poison?) - but now we did. Our children survived accordingly (they just glow in the dark, ha ha).

Even if you're not a person of faith, there's something to be said for raising your kids to develop physical - and mental - resilience against sickness, rather than giving in to the first sniffle or sneeze.

A legendary parental response came from the father of a friend of ours. She would occasionally feel a little off-colour and request a day off school. Her dad would ask her, "Have you vomited?" to which she would reply "No, but…". "Well, you're fine then" he would say, "go to school". One day, she felt so sick she actually *did* vomit, and thought *well finally I'll be getting a day off*. She told her father she was unwell, to which he rolled out his standard "Have you vomited?". This time, our friend was able to reply "yes, Dad, I *have* vomited". But without a moment's hesitation, he shot back "Well, in that case you'll be fine now - go to school". She just couldn't win. But in the end she did - with a strong immune system and expectation of good health.

Ok so that's an extreme example, and I'm not proposing that you copy this! We need to follow our own instincts, with wisdom, care and kindness. But that old-school parenting was training his kids to have a strong mindset about health. Whichever way you go about it, help your kids learn how to fight in the battle against sickness. Use medicine when required, build healthy lifestyle habits, lead them to be strong and teach them the power of prayer. At least two of our kids had situations that could easily have led to something serious if we simply accepted the initial diagnoses. But we fought for their health with positivity and prayer. You can do the same. Don't just hope for health - believe for it.

CREATE ROUTINES

Children feel safer and more secure when their world is predictable.
- Dr. Laura Markham

n 2023, researchers from Colorado State University published a study in the journal *Brain and Behaviour*, examining the effects of family routines on child development. They observed children aged five to nine from a range of backgrounds and looked at the presence - or absence - of regular routines like bedtime rituals, shared mealtimes, reading before bed, and morning schedules. MRI scans revealed that kids with more stable routines slept longer, and better sleep was linked to enhanced development in areas of the brain responsible for language, sensory perception and emotional regulation. This supports other research showing that children and teens who consistently get at least eight hours of sleep perform better on cognitive tests than those with disrupted sleep patterns.[1]

Family routines are important - they create a rhythm to life that helps kids feel safe, secure and stable. Children are more likely to be confident and relaxed when they know what's coming next. Things like:

- Daily routines: getting up and ready for school, goodbyes and greetings, bath and dinner time, bedtime prep.
- Weekly routines: chores, family nights, Church, sport on the weekend.
- Special routines: family birthdays, holiday traditions, regular catch-ups with extended family.

Routines help everyone understand what's important and who's doing what, when and how. They keep family life functional without being rigid - there's still room for flexibility, like staying up late for Christmas lights or a dinner outing.

For us, when the kids were young, we always gave them a five-minute warning before bedtime. Then it was straight into the "teeth, toilet, bed" song (Ruth had a tune for most things). There was never any drama because it was just part of the daily routine. Our older kids claim we sent everyone to bed at the same time regardless of age, which they say is unfair - especially when they found out their mates stayed up much later. I, of course, have no memory of this and choose to believe we ran a perfectly fair and balanced operation.

There's solid science behind regular bedtimes too. A University College London study in 2013 followed 11,000 kids and found that irregular sleep times were linked to lower scores in reading, maths, and spatial awareness. This was consistent with studies from other countries, including Australia. The recommendation? Kids aged three to five need around 11–12 hours per night, and primary schoolers need about 10 - 11 hours.[2]

So yes, routines might seem boring or structured at times, but they're one of the unsung heroes of parenting. They take the chaos out of daily life, build healthy habits for the long haul, and create an environment where kids can flourish.

⚙ ENDNOTES

[1] Merz, E. C., Rosen, M. L., Kaplan, A. R., Friedman, A., Lenker, C., & McLaughlin, K. A. (2023). Socioeconomic disparities in sleep duration are associated with cortical thickness in children. *Brain and Behavior, 13*(2), e2894. https://doi.org/10.1002/brb3.2894

[2] Kelly, Y., Kelly, J., & Sacker, A. (2013). Changes in bedtime schedules and behavioral difficulties in 7-year-old children. *Pediatrics, 132*(5), e1184–e1193. https://doi.org/10.1542/peds.2013-1906

BUILD A GREAT MARRIAGE

If you want to raise secure kids, start by building a secure marriage. Kids don't need perfection, but they do need parents who choose love and loyalty every day.

\- Ian Grant

Parenting experts around the world - including Ian Grant from New Zealand, quoted above - agree that the best foundation for raising happy, healthy children is a strong, stable marriage. Of course, kids are resilient, and they'll manage in broken and blended families, but if you're married, stick with it. Hopefully, not just "for the sake of the kids", but because it's worth it for you two as well.

I'm not writing a marriage manual, but after observing families over the years, I'm convinced that most failed marriages could have been rescued - and not just back to survival mode, but to something rich and rewarding. I've met a number of people on their second or third marriage who admit that their previous union would have been a lot better if they applied what they know now.

A good marriage needs maintenance and investment. Men, think of it like a classic car or motorbike (true romance!) - if you don't look after it, things seize up and fall apart. But with regular care and attention, it can run beautifully for years to come.

Here are just a few of the key benefits that a strong, loving marriage provides for children:

Emotional security.

Kids thrive in a stable, loving home environment. Dr. John Gottman, a leading relationship researcher, found that conflict-ridden or emotionally distant marriages increase a child's stress and anxiety levels, while healthy, affectionate marriages help children feel safe and grounded. He writes that when parents model respectful conflict resolution and affection, children learn how to manage emotions and relationships.[1]

Healthy relationship modelling.

Your marriage is the first relationship your kids see up close. It becomes their blueprint for how to love, communicate, and resolve conflict. In *The 5 Love Languages of Children*, Dr Gary Chapman writes, "A loving, supportive marriage models for children how to build lasting relationships based on love, respect and commitment".[2] Your kids are watching - and learning - every day.

Economic and practical stability.

A strong marriage provides a more stable environment for raising kids. Finances are typically healthier, time management is easier, and emotional support for parenting is available for each other. There's nothing better after a challenging day raising little kids than for the main stay-at-home carer to hand the kids over to their spouse arriving home from work; "here, they're all yours, I'm going for a walk".

Reduced stress.

When parents are in a loving and supportive relationship, there's less tension in the home, and more peace. That doesn't mean an absence of conflict, but it does mean that the two adults learn how to resolve the conflict. And don't feel like you need to hide every disagreement from your kids. Obviously, some issues are best dealt with privately, but sometimes it's appropriate and helpful to let them see you work out your differences - it equips them to do the same in the future.

In the end, one of the greatest gifts you can give your children is a loving, lasting marriage. Not a perfect one, but one marked by commitment, kindness, and consistent effort. When your kids grow up in a home where love is modelled and security is felt, they carry that strength with them into every other area of life. Building a great marriage will build a great foundation for your future family.

⚙ ENDNOTES

[1] John M. Gottman and Lynn Fainsilber Katz, "Patterns of Marital Conflict Predict Children's Internalizing and Externalizing Behaviors," *Developmental Psychology* 29, no. 6 (1993): 940–950; and John M. Gottman with Joan DeClaire, *Raising an Emotionally Intelligent Child: The Heart of Parenting* (New York: Simon & Schuster, 1997).

[2] Gary Chapman and Ross Campbell, *The 5 Love Languages of Children: The Secret to Loving Children Effectively* (Chicago: Northfield Publishing, 1997).

BE DISCIPLINED ABOUT DISCIPLINE

Train up a child in the way he should go and
when he is old he will not turn from it
- Proverbs 22:6

You can only expect children to behave in line with what they understand. If a crawling baby knocks over a precious ornament and breaks it, that's not disobedience - that's your cue to move breakables out of reach. But when your child is old enough to know they shouldn't touch something, and they do it anyway, that's when a lesson needs to be taught.

Some parents go too hard too soon, expecting their kids to behave like miniature adults. Others are too soft, never setting any clear boundaries, and ending up with a little tyrant running (and ruining) the household. Neither extreme helps your child.

As soon as your kids are old enough to understand, begin showing them what you expect. Keep it simple and age-appropriate, such as:

- say please and thank you
- hold my hand when we cross the road
- always tell the truth
- don't hit your sister

Don't expect the impossible, like telling a three-year-old to sit still and quiet for an hour while you chat with a friend in a café. Or that your toddler will keep their clothes perfectly clean when playing in the backyard. But do set firm, clear expectations of their behaviour - that grow as they grow. Compare notes with other parents. See how other families operate. Most importantly, discuss with your wife what the two of you agree on for your own kids - discipline needs consistency and teamwork.

When your child does cross the line, take time to understand why. Maybe it was forgetfulness, or a moment of foolishness, rather than wilful disobedience or rebellion. Simple mistakes don't warrant punishment. Sometimes a gentle reminder or redirection is enough. Mix wisdom and grace into your behavioural boundary setting - kids need to feel safe and loved, even when they've missed it. It's far better to raise children who feel secure in your love, and enjoy being around you, than to rule the house with fear and constant correction. A home full of laughter, fun and connection makes discipline easier, because kids won't be misbehaving just to get your attention.

Of course, when (not if) your child knowingly breaks the rules, don't ignore it. Follow through with consequences for misbehaviour and help them get back on track. By the time your child is a toddler, they need to learn what's right and wrong, and they won't naturally pick that up without your help. Be firm, be fair, be consistent. And never forget, you're raising a person, not just managing a problem.

READ AND TELL STORIES

If you want your children to be intelligent, read them fairy tales.
If you want them to be more intelligent, read them more fairy tales.
- Albert Einstein

t's never too early to start reading to your kids or telling them stories. Not only is it fun, but there's plenty of research that shows it boosts child development, even when they're babies - and incredibly, even while they're still in the womb. Some of these benefits are that it:

- helps healthy brain development.
- builds connection and bonding between parent and child.
- expands vocabulary and speeds up language learning.

- aids emotional development, by building empathy with characters in stories.
- prepares kids for learning to read.
- assists social development, by providing communication patterns to follow.
- fuels creativity by helping kids picture things in their mind.[1]

That last point has become even more valuable in today's screen-heavy world. So many children are constantly entertained with moving images, sound effects, and apps that do all the imagining for them. But a simple spoken story - especially one without pictures - invites kids to create the scene in their own mind. That builds imagination - by letting the brain do the work, instead of outsourcing it to a screen.

Reading kids' books can also be a real win-win, in that you get to enjoy them as well. Ok, I admit that *Where's Spot* might test your sanity after the 400th read (I've been there), but who hasn't loved *Where the Wild Things Are* or just about any Dr Seuss story?

Another benefit is that many stories come with a built-in moral lesson, which opens the door to discussions about right and wrong, honour, courage and other ethical issues you want your kids to consider. This is especially true if you make up your own stories - you can personalise them by including your own kids, weaving in recent events, and giving them your own version of an ancient Greek morality play.

For my kids growing up I created "Nigel the Ant". I couldn't tell you the origin of this character, but he was the everyman/ant hero of the backyard kingdom, who went on various adventures, including paying for human teeth he found in glasses of water at night which his King would use for ivory gates in the palace (our version of the tooth fairy). Others had a moral lesson hidden within the story - well, when I say hidden, it was usually pretty obvious, like Nigel being commended by the King for his bravery or kindness to another insect.

Remember - story time is great connection time. When your kids sit on your lap, together you can head off into other worlds, dream, talk, cuddle, calm down at the end of a busy day, and prepare for bed - all in ten minutes. That's a big return on the investment.

⚙ ENDNOTES

[1] NSW Health. *Reading to babies and very young children.* Sydney: NSW Government, November 2018.

MEAN WHAT YOU SAY

Well done is better than well said
- Benjamin Franklin

As the saying goes, "Be a man of your word". Sadly, some blokes - even with good intentions - talk things up, but don't deliver. That kind of inconsistency sends a confusing message to kids. Your children should be able to rely on your word. Don't let them grow up wondering whether Dad actually means what he says or not.

A few examples of following through on what you say to your kids include:

• **Disciplining with consistency.**

If you've warned your kids about consequences for inappropriate behaviour, don't back down when it's time to back up what you spoke about. How many times have you heard a parent count to three, only to discover that nothing happens at three? Or they slow down the count because they're reluctant to act:

"One…. (pause)……Two…(long pause)…. two and a half… (longer pause)… I mean it… ….Two-point-seven-five (excruciatingly-even-longer pause)….. don't make me get to three….(this-is-now-getting-ridiculous pause)….. two-point-eight-four…."

This just teaches the kid that the warnings don't mean much, and that boundaries are negotiable.

- **Giving the "5 minute warning" at the playground.**

It's often too jarring for a kid to hear "Let's go, we're leaving" when they're in the middle of their game. So, you give them a heads-up: "Five more minutes, then we're going". That's a good strategy, as long as five minutes doesn't become twenty-five, or the start of negotiations - if so, respect for your authority is lost.

And do yourself a favour: never play the "I'm going now!" game. You know the one - when you start walking off pretending to leave, hoping your toddler will come running after you. This either traumatizes the kid at the thought of being abandoned, or - as is usually the case - teaches them that Dad's threats are empty. Either way, they learn that Dad doesn't really mean what he says - and worse - that they're in charge.

- **Fulfilling promises.**

Be careful with the words, "I promise". Whether it's making it to their footy game, watching their school play, or taking them to the beach on the weekend - only say it if you're sure you can follow through. There'll be times when you hope to make it, but have other commitments (no, that doesn't mean watching TV is more important than supporting your child's acting debut). So, if you're uncertain, just be upfront, and speak honestly: "I'm hoping to make it your game, but I might be working", or "If we can't get to the beach on Saturday, don't worry, we'll try for Sunday arvo".

But when you can promise - then do it properly. Prioritise it and diarise it. Lock in the appointment with your kid and honour it, just as you would with an adult. Following through builds trust, encourages your kids, and lets them know how important they are to you.

Your kids need to know your words matter - that they are to be trusted, listened to, and obeyed. So don't bluff. Don't bargain. Don't say things you don't mean. Let your yes be yes. Be the kind of dad whose words are strong, steady, dependable, and backed up by action.

★ DRAW WITH THEM ★

*Every child is an artist. The problem is how to
remain an artist once we grow up*
- Pablo Picasso

Y ou don't need to be a gifted artist to pick up a crayon and join your
kids at the table. Drawing, scribbling, colouring, painting, sketching
pictures - whatever form it takes, it's good for the soul. For children,

art is more than just a fun activity; it's a natural way to express their thoughts and feelings, especially when words don't quite cut it.

Drawing and other art forms boosts creativity, sharpens motor skills, supports emotional development and increases the ability to concentrate on a task. It's even used by child psychologists as a form of therapy. Giving kids a blank page and a box of pencils is like handing them a passport to explore their inner world.

And don't just hand them the art supplies and walk away - sit down and draw with them. It's a great way to bond with your kids, and you'll be surprised at the conversations you have when there's no pressure or agenda - not to mention re-discovering your artistic talents.

It's also a cheap, simple and screen-free form of entertainment. The drawing or painting may end up proudly displayed on the fridge, but the real goal isn't the finished product - it's all about being present, tuning in, and enjoying the journey of creativity together.

Tips for drawing together:

- No pressure, no perfection. Let go of needing to "draw well" and having rules to follow. It's not about talent, it's about expression.
- Mix it up. Don't stop with paper and pencils. Try chalk on the driveway, finger painting, collages with leaves and sticks, modelling clay, papier-mâché, modelling with recycled materials - the list goes on.
- Be curious, not critical. Ask open-ended questions that open the door to their thoughts without making them feel judged. Try "tell me about your drawing" rather than, "What is it?"

- Show it off. Stick their masterpiece on the fridge, put it in a frame, or give it pride of place somewhere else: "It's going straight to the pool room!"

My office currently has a wall covered in pictures drawn by the grandies when they visit (I keep coloured pencils and paper handy in a drawer). It's a simple way to say, "What you create matters - and you matter".

FOSTER CREATIVITY

Creativity takes courage
- Henri Matisse

As your children get older, you will be the best person to notice their gifts and help them shine.

I've already mentioned how I lost a few tools when the boys were out building tree houses around the neighbourhood. At one point I drove loads of recycled timber up into the bush for them to build a crazy construction way up in the trees. But it was all worth it to support such a healthy, creative pastime.

One of our daughters created an 'art corner' in the workshop next to the tools. The hand-painted sign on the wall is still there, and there's been all kinds of art and craft activities going on there over the years.

Our daughter Ellena had a penchant for writing, even from a young age. We encouraged it, and take full credit for her successful career as a professional writer.

Take your kids to plays, art galleries and music concerts (your teenagers will be happy to spend a night out with you if you're shouting them a ticket to something cool - just bring your earplugs if they're into screamo stuff).

Speaking of screamo music - one of our boys got into that in his teens. We made the effort to listen and support his artistic choice - and occasionally understood a word that was sung. Whatever they're into - even if it's not your cup of tea - give them the respect they deserve for developing their personal taste in the arts.

Also let your kids experiment with their appearance. We always drew the line at tattoos, because they're so permanent, but otherwise allowed our kids increasing freedom as they grew up in terms of how they wanted to present themselves. Fashion is a great way to let them enjoy fairly low-stakes creative expression. We endured many questionable hairstyles during the teen years – bleached-white blonde, mohawks, mullets, and dreadlocks - all a bit crazy but 'normal' hair can always grow back. More than one of our kids dyed their hair blue, which we were ok with, but I was less excited when their after-school boredom led them to dye the back of our small white dog blue! (Thankfully he was due for a haircut, so it didn't last long. And he seemed to enjoy the attention).

How many of us as adults have said, "I've always wanted to play guitar." or "I used to love art at school, I wish I stuck with it!" We have the benefit of hindsight, so let's give our kids every opportunity to explore and enjoy their creativity.

NORMAL IS FINE

There is only one pretty child in the world, and every mother has it.
- Chinese Proverb

Ever wondered where the normal kids are?

Everyone's child seems advanced - especially if they're first-time parents who are obsessively tracking every metric of their kid's development. Throw in a bit of social media, some parental comparison and a dash of competitiveness and suddenly it looks like your child is way behind where they should be. I remember one little boy who didn't talk for years. By the time he was three or four, while others were chatting away in the sandpit, he'd just point and grunt, like he had as a baby. His parents were worried about serious developmental delays. But sure enough, his speech kicked in eventually, and he grew up to be bright, articulate and a brilliant schoolteacher. The lesson? Don't panic. Don't compete. Don't compare. Developmental milestones vary widely. Kids develop language, motor and social skills at different paces - and most will catch up without the need for any intervention.

It's also important not to put pressure on your child to be the best, brightest or the most well-behaved all the time. Expecting brilliance can quietly crush kids under the weight of unrealistic expectations. As parenting author Elizabeth Hartley-Brewer warns:

"We're in danger of creating a society hamstrung by perfectionism where the 'successful' pay a heavy price in terms of their emotional health, and the 'unsuccessful' are socially excluded."[1]

Striving for excellence is one thing, but idolizing it is another. Failure isn't a flaw - it's part of life. Kids need the freedom to mess up, miss out and learn the hard way. They also don't need a medal for just getting dressed in the morning. If we constantly reward the most basic behaviour - like getting out of bed or showing up to school - we can create a distorted view of reality. Every waking moment of a child's life shouldn't be showered with attention and accolades - if so, when they actually do achieve something praiseworthy, the award or recognition will carry far less weight.

The truth is, not every child is destined to be a gifted genius, a pop star, or a household name. Plenty of people live rich, meaningful, successful lives without ever standing on a podium, or trending online. Some are truly great, while never being famous. Your child might be one of them - and that's ok - it's normal.

⚙ ENDNOTES

[1] Elizabeth Hartley-Brewer, *Raising a Self-Starter* (Cambridge, MA: Da Capo Press, 2004).

TEACH THEM MANNERS

Politeness is the flower of humanity.
- Joseph Joubert

N o one's born with good manners - but they're one of the best things a kid can learn. We all appreciate it when people say and do the right thing. Manners are the basic social glue that help us all get along in society.

There are certain unspoken expectations in life that open doors - not just socially, but professionally. No matter how clever he is, a genius won't land the job if he's rude, badly dressed, and slouching in the interview. But someone with average skills and a friendly, polite manner will often go further than they expected. As U.S. Supreme Court Justice Clarence Thomas once said, *"Good manners will open doors that the best education cannot."*

So, teach your kids how to:

Look someone in the eye and say hello.

When they're being greeted by someone, insist they respond politely. Don't excuse them with "Oh she's shy" or "Isn't that cute?" when they run off without replying.

Use good table manners:

Chew with your mouth closed, don't reach across the table, say "please" when asking for something, ask to leave the table rather than just walk away. (I could go on; my Air Force Officer dad used to say, "What if you're dining at the officer's mess - or with royalty?" - I'm still waiting for an invitation).

Hold a conversation.

Kids can learn early on to answer with more than a grunt, and to ask simple questions like, "How was your day?".

Clean themselves up.

Wash regularly, brush their teeth, comb their hair, and get dressed without being chased around the house.

Speak respectfully to adults.

"Yes please", "No thank you" and "Excuse me" go a long way - especially when speaking to teachers, relatives or shopkeepers. And don't let your kids interrupt your conversation easily - when they're dying to say something, teach them to wait (but not for too long), and then excuse yourself briefly to hear from your child. Just hold up your hand, and your kids will come to learn that it means, "I'll be with you in a moment, but I'm busy right now".

Welcome others.

"Hi, nice to meet you?" or "Want to play with us?" are simple phrases that help children include others.

Everytime they see their grandfather, run to him, throw their arms around him and say, "Grandad, you're amazing!" (I'm hoping my kids buy this book).

Manners tend to match what's going on inside someone. If you're mean and nasty, you can only put on a polite front for so long. But forming habits that treat people well can actually improve your character. As we've said before, educating our children starts with us as parents, and it's not just about imparting information - it's about preparing them for life. So, aim to build into your kids not just polite behaviour, but character that goes along with it: qualities like love, forgiveness, grace, wisdom, honour, courage, and respect. As American President Theodore Roosevelt once said: *"To educate a person in the mind but not in morals is to educate a menace to society."*

Manners matter.

ENROY THE ENERGY

★ **ENJOY THE ENERGY** ★

The soul is healed by being with children.
- Fyodor Dostoyevsky

We've all seen - and probably been - the parent struggling in public with a little one who seems to have an endless supply of energy. It's not always misbehaviour; sometimes it's just kids doing what comes naturally - running up and down the supermarket aisle, chasing siblings inside a friend's house, or yelling at the top of their lungs in places that were not designed for yelling. Ever tried to quieten your kids in a library with a 'whisper shout'? "Kids! Be quiet!", you hiss, ironically louder than they were in the first place.

Of course, toddlers and pre-schoolers need to learn how to behave appropriately in different settings. But they also need opportunities to let loose. Kids aren't made to sit still all day. Their bodies are wired to move, explore and burn off energy - not just for fun, but for healthy development.

Research has proven that physical activity not only improves kids' movement skills, but also their mood, emotional regulation, sleep, brain development and attention span.[1] Children who are given regular opportunities to be active are less likely to act out and more likely to thrive in structured environments like school. Good teachers know this and make use of "movement breaks" to help their students return to focus on academic work.

So instead of constantly trying to calm your kids down, find the right place and time to let them run wild. Take them outside - the backyard, a park, the beach, or your local playground - anywhere that suits running, jumping, screaming and generally going nuts. And when you've found the right place, don't just supervise - enjoy it. Laugh, cheer, and even join in.

If we're always telling our kids to sit still and be quiet, we risk suppressing not just their energy, but their zest for life. Worse still, we can unintentionally communicate that their natural enthusiasm is a problem to be managed rather than a gift to be celebrated.

Remember, your kids' energy is not a burden - it's a blessing - and it might just rub off on you.

ENDNOTES

[1] Be You. (n.d.). *Physical activity and mental health and wellbeing.* https://beyou.edu.au/resources/fact-sheets/physical-activity-and-mental-health-and-wellbeing

OUT IN PUBLIC

Praise your children openly, reprove them secretly.
- William Cecil.

aking young kids out in public can be a bit of an adventure - and occasionally a circus. But it doesn't have to be a disaster. With some forethought, clear communication, and well-timed encouragement, you can help your kids learn how to behave well in public while still giving them room to explore and enjoy the world. Here' s some basic guidelines:

Set the Expectations

Life's a lot easier when your kids know the plan. Before you step into a shopping centre, café, or park, let them know the basic expectations:

- Stay close
- Speak kindly
- Don't touch without asking
- Be respectful of others

Kids are also entitled to know what's going on. Tell them where you're going, why you're going there, and roughly how long you'll be.

The Treat Talk

A classic trap is the shopping treat. Decide *beforehand* whether or not you're buying something for them. Maybe today it's a reward for helping with the groceries. Maybe you're having a "treat-free" day (especially important if treats have become so common they're no longer treats). Either way, *tell them ahead of time* and stick to it. If you say no to a donut twelve times, but then give in on the thirteenth, guess what you've just taught your child? That nagging pays off. Consistency builds trust, and it means there's no exhausting power struggles every time you go near a shop.

Dealing with Misbehaviour

Discipline in public can be awkward, but it's necessary. If your child is hitting, yelling, running wild or being unkind, you can't just ignore it - nor is it fair to say, "Wait till we get home," especially with younger kids. Educational psychologists agree that young children respond best when consequences happen *immediately*, so they can connect the dots between what they did and the deterrent that followed. But you don't have to make a big scene. If needed, remove your child to a quieter spot - around the corner, or outside the shop - and deal with it privately, whether it's just a few words or something a little stronger. Keep calm, reminding them not only what *not* to do, but also what *to* do.

Keep an Eye on the Good Stuff

While it's easy to spot the bad behaviour, don't forget to catch your kids doing the *right* thing too. If they wait patiently in line, use kind words with a sibling, or stay close just as you asked - then say something encouraging and positive to them. A quiet "Thanks for being so helpful" or a proud "I noticed you waited really patiently back there" goes a long way.

Children thrive on praise. It's like fuel for their confidence. And when they feel secure and seen, they're far more likely to behave well.

Let Them Explore (safely)

Outings aren't just about managing behaviour - they're about learning too. So let your kids explore, ask questions, and interact with the world. Just make sure the boundaries are clear:

- "You can walk beside the trolley, but you need to stay near me."
- "You can look at the toys, but we're not buying anything today."

Good parenting isn't about constant control - it's about *safe freedom*. Let them know you're watching, and you care, without hovering and worrying.

Your kids will make mistakes. They'll forget the rules. They'll complain. They'll touch something they shouldn't. But every public outing is a learning opportunity. When you set clear expectations, stay consistent with discipline, and hand out praise, your kids will learn how to navigate the world respectfully and confidently.

SCREEN POLICING

Technology can be our best friend, but it can also
be the biggest party pooper of our lives.
It interrupts our own story.
- Steven Spielberg

Too many kids are glued to screens - and there's a lot of glue. When I was a kid the only screen you could get addicted to was black and white television. And there wasn't much to choose from - just afternoon repeats of *Batman, Lost in Space,* or *The Bugs Bunny Show.* These days, children are spoiled for choice - and sometimes overwhelmed by it. They're surrounded by entertainment on every kind of device: streaming services, smartphones, tablets, computers, and gaming consoles - they don't even need a TV.

And it's not just about the *amount* of content - it's about the *kind* of content that's available, and the effect it has on our kids. Here are a few of the biggest challenges:

- **Inappropriate content:** From violence and explicit material to toxic attitudes and misinformation, there's a lot online that kids shouldn't see.
- **Addiction to gaming and scrolling:** Many games and platforms are designed to be addictive, keeping kids engaged with endless scrolling, reward loops, and dopamine hits.

- **Cyberbullying and social media stress:** Social media can be brutal, especially for young minds still forming their identity and resilience.
- **Withdrawal from real-world relationships:** Too much screen time can lead to social disconnection, poor communication skills, and less time outdoors or playing creatively. This has become even more of an issue with AI chat-bots simulating real conversations.

Most kids (and many adults) don't naturally limit their screen time. That's for you to help them with. Be a gatekeeper. Before smartphones, it was a lot easier to monitor what kids were doing online. Families often had a shared desktop in a common area, and you could keep an eye on what was going on. But now, with kids carrying screens in their pockets, it's much trickier. Some families delay giving their kids a personal device until they're well into high school. And for good reason - up to now, most social media platforms set 13 as the minimum age. But as I write this, legislation in Australia is now moving to raise that to 16. That's a clear sign that even governments are starting to take the risks seriously.

There are technical tools - filters, blockers, parental control apps - that can help limit exposure to inappropriate content. But no tool is foolproof, and clever kids often find their way around them. That's why many experts, including those from the Australian eSafety Commissioner, agree that the most effective strategy includes education, supervision and relationship.[1]

So, talk to your kids. Help them understand what's out there - the good, the bad, and the ugly. Teach them self-control, personal boundaries, and how to make wise choices when no one's watching. Discuss with your kids the effect of advertising and online influencers, so they can develop critical thinking and exercise their own will and choice, rather than just being sucked in by whatever's promoted through media.

Of course, not everything on a screen is evil. In recent years, when I go into a school as a casual teacher, I've noticed the growth in excellent educational resources on the internet - from maths games to reading programs and science tutorials. The internet is also full of creative tools that kids can use to explore, invent, and learn. The trick is helping your children engage actively, not just consume passively.

We also shouldn't forget the role of entertainment. There's plenty of wholesome, fun programs and shows for kids to enjoy.

Here are a few screen-time strategies that worked for us:

- **No screens in the morning.** Mornings are prime time for getting ready, tidying rooms, and starting the day well. TV just slows everything down.
- **TV off during dinner.** Mealtimes are for connection. It's a great time to talk about your day, not stare at a screen.
- **Time limits help.** When screen time is limited, kids appreciate it more. Watching a favourite show becomes a treat, not a default activity.
- **Use screens intentionally.** Whether it's watching a movie together or playing an educational game, make screen time something you share with your kids.
- **Phones away in the evening.** Especially as kids move into teen years and social media becomes more of a thing, it's best to ensure all devices are kept out of their bedrooms.

You don't need to be a tech expert - just an involved parent. Set boundaries. Have conversations. And be willing to say no sometimes. Remember: screens should serve your family - not run it.

⚙ ENDNOTES

[1] eSafety Commissioner. (n.d.). *Parental controls | How to keep your child safe.* eSafety Commissioner. Retrieved 8 September 2025, from https://www.esafety.gov.au/parents/issues-and-advice/parental-controls

TRUTH TELLING

★   ★

Truth is like a lion. You don't have to defend it.
Let it loose - it will defend itself.
- Augustine of Hippo

The truth is powerful, wonderful, and foundational to a functional family. In a world that often blurs the lines, teaching your kids to value truth is one of the greatest gifts we can give them.

We want our kids to recognize the truth, appreciate it, and enjoy telling it - even when it's hard. That kind of honesty doesn't just happen on its own. It takes deliberate modelling, consistent encouragement, and fair but firm boundaries.

School

One place this really matters is at school. It's normal for children to hold back on some of what goes on there, and to be nervous about admitting when they've messed up. But being informed is essential. You can't help your child improve their behaviour - or protect them from unfair blame - if they're too afraid to tell you the full story.

That's why trust matters. If your kids know you won't come down on them like a tonne of bricks for every minor misdemeanour, they're far more likely to be open and honest. That doesn't mean you excuse the behaviour or let them off the hook (*"Don't worry dear, we've all wanted to set fire to the school at some point"*). What it means is that you respond fairly - with appropriate consequences, but also with grace, belief, and love. *"I'm proud of you for telling me the truth. And yes, you're still grounded, because schools aren't meant to go up in flames... but I appreciate your honesty."*

Psychologist Dr. Nancy Darling has researched factors that influence honesty in kids and found that they're more likely to tell the truth when parents respond in ways that are warm, fair, and consistent - not overly harsh or dismissive.[1]

When kids don't speak up

Sometimes kids stay silent, even when they're not the guilty ones. One of our boys went through a season of being lumped in with the "usual suspects" at school. Occasionally, he'd take the fall for things he hadn't even started - especially when other boys were quick to point fingers. He'd shut down, accept the punishment, and we'd only hear the full story much later. In those situations, you want your child to feel safe enough to speak up. Teach them that telling the truth matters, even when it's awkward or hard. Not just to avoid unfair punishment, but to grow in integrity.

Honesty about doing the wrong thing

Let's be real - most kids will lie at some point to avoid getting in trouble. That's why it's crucial we insist on the truth and hold the line. I've been a teacher long enough to see what happens when that doesn't occur. Some parents struggle to accept that their perfect angel of a child could possibly be at fault - for anything. Instead of confronting the behaviour, they'll blame the teacher, the school, other students, or anyone else they can think of. That's not helping their kid. Wise parents work with the school, listen carefully, and expect full honesty from their children. The goal isn't punishment - it's character.

Fantasy vs falsehood

Little kids live in a magical world where teddy bears require dinner and dragons show up in the backyard. That's part of the fun of childhood. But at some point, they need help distinguishing between fantasy and reality. A gentle correction can work wonders: *"Wow, that's a brilliant story! But that didn't actually happen, right?"* Left unchecked, some kids develop the habit of exaggeration or outright lying to impress others. What's cute at 4 can become awkward at 10, and sad at 16. A child who doesn't learn the value of truth may grow into an adult who struggles with honesty in relationships, work, or life.

Speaking of fantasy, we decided not to teach our kids that Santa or The Easter Bunny were real - they were (and are - spoiler alert) just fun characters - like Mickey Mouse. I know that plenty of families still run with this as a fun game, but we didn't want to tell our children something was true if it really wasn't - and there was still plenty of fun and fantasy to enjoy.

Build a Culture of Truth at Home

Stamp out lying - but also build up honesty. Praise your kids when they tell the truth, especially when it's hard. That's how you reinforce integrity. For example, you find your 6-year-old with a shiny new toy car after visiting a mate's house:

"Did you take this from Michael without asking?"

"Yes..."

"Okay. That's stealing, and that's wrong. You're going to return it and apologise. But well done for being honest."

The Ultimate Truth

We live in a world where half-truths, spin, and fake news are everywhere. But as parents, we can give our kids a different, stronger, truthful foundation. Not just by telling them to speak the truth - but by living it, modelling it, and valuing it ourselves. Remind them of the words of Jesus: *"You will know the truth, and the truth will set you free."* - John 8:32. Because it really does.

⚙ ENDNOTES

[1]   Darling, N. (2025, May 15). *Busted! Does punishment teach kids to lie?* GreatSchools.org. Retrieved from https://www.greatschools.org/gk/parenting/social-emotional-learning/busted-lying-and-punishment

WORK IS GOOD

He who does not teach his son a trade teaches him to steal.
- Jewish proverb

From making their bed to mowing the lawn, work teaches kids more than just how to do a task - it builds character. Giving kids jobs around the house helps them grow in responsibility, self-discipline, and contributes to a strong work ethic that will serve them for the rest of their lives.

You can start giving kids chores from the age of three or four - even if their "help" leaves more mess than you started with. By the time they're in school - ages five or six - regular household jobs should be part of the normal rhythm of family life. It teaches them that home isn't a hotel: we all live here, and we all contribute.

By the primary years, it's a win-win: the kids are learning the value of work *and* genuinely helping out. Things like washing up, setting the table, tidying their room, sweeping the floor, weeding the garden, and feeding the pets are all jobs that build life skills and lighten the load for parents.

Work doesn't always need to be rewarded with money - nor should it be. We found it helpful to distinguish between two types of jobs:

- Family responsibilities: these are unpaid chores that everyone pitches in on.
- Optional jobs for pocket money: extra tasks the kids can choose to do for a reward.

Avoid two extremes: one, where you're so stingy the kids never learn the satisfaction of earning, the other, where the parents splash the cash for very little work. Let your children experience the right connection between effort, time, and reward.

If you don't build this culture of contribution in their primary years, you may find yourself ranting at teenagers with cries of "This is not a hotel, you know!" as they saunter around the house, blind to their own mess and allergic to the idea of lifting a finger. That can (usually) be avoided if you start early, build healthy habits, and normalise work as part of family life.

Young kids often *want* to help. They love being a part of your cooking, cleaning and tidying. Of course, it's quicker to do it all yourself, but involving them at this early stage helps create a sense of value and belonging. So let them help and praise their efforts; "Thanks, the kitchen looks so much better now," or "Great job - you're such a good helper". This builds more than helpful habits - it nurtures a mindset of *intrinsic satisfaction,* where work is worthwhile, even without external rewards.

When they're old enough, a part-time job outside the home is a great next step. It strengthens their sense of independence, teaches responsibility, and helps them appreciate the relationship between work and money. It also gives them a taste of what a boss expects and how the world works.

Some kids are natural go-getters. One of ours, Keighlan, was already hustling for work before he was 10. He found an old wagon in a roadside clean-up and turned it into his mobile shop, selling his Nan's handmade soaps and candles around the neighbourhood. At 14, he landed a job at Maccas, worked his way into extra shifts, then started a carpentry apprenticeship at 16, which he finished by 18 (and 11 months - oh I may have mentioned this before #proudfather). Not all kids are so keen to work (and leave school), but there's some kind of casual work that will suit each kid, and they'll be better for it.

Statistics reveal that nearly half of Australia's school students aged 16 -17 are in some kind of part-time paid employment[1], and research shows that teens who work moderate hours (under 15 a week) often develop better time management and responsibility skills than those who don't[2].

Teaching kids to save is a natural extension of teaching them to work. We started with small deposits into school savings accounts in the early years. Later, in high school, we set up two bank accounts: one for short-term goals (like a game or bike), and one longer-term account, which was named the "Car account.". My philosophy was simple: I won't buy you a car, but I'll help if you save for one. That way, they learned delayed gratification and valued what they'd worked for, as well as maintaining the car better than if it was just a gift. We matched their savings dollar-for-dollar for a while… until some of them got a little *too* enthusiastic, and we had to renegotiate terms before I went broke.

Work for kids is more than just getting chores done - it's preparing them well for the future. Helping out at home builds the kind of resilience, responsibility, and readiness that sets them up for life. They learn that effort has value. That contribution matters. And that they're not the centre of the universe, but an important part of a team. As Thomas Edison said, *"Opportunity is missed by most people because it is dressed in overalls and looks like work."* So, start early. Give them the gift of learning how to work - not just because it helps you around the house, but because it helps *them* grow into capable, contributing adults.

⚙ ENDNOTES

[1] Australian Bureau of Statistics. (2023). *Schools, Australia, 2022.* Canberra: ABS. Retrieved from https://www.abs.gov.au/statistics/people/education/schools/latest-release

[2] Australian Institute of Family Studies. (2021). *Adolescents combining school and part-time employment.* Growing Up in Australia Snapshot Series – Issue 6. Retrieved from https://aifs.gov.au/growing-australia/research/research-snapshots/adolescents-combining-school-and-part-time-employment

GIVING IS GREAT

No one has ever become poor by giving.
- Anne Frank

Generosity is one of the most powerful values we can help our kids develop - not just the act of giving money or possessions, but cultivating a generous spirit. It's about raising kids who are kind-hearted, open-handed, and willing to share their time, attention, and energy with others.

For primary-aged children, generosity can take many forms: sharing their toys, giving up the last piece of cake, helping a friend with a school project, or spending time with a lonely classmate during lunch. These moments might seem small and insignificant, but their impact on character can be huge. It helps kids learn that they're capable of making a difference in someone else's world. That sense of agency is powerful - it builds empathy and confidence, and they grow up knowing that their actions matter.

Research backs this up. Studies in child development have shown that generosity fosters empathy, builds stronger social bonds, and even boosts happiness. A 2012 study from the University of British Columbia found that children as young as two experienced greater happiness when they gave treats to others rather than receiving them themselves.[1]

Scientific research also shows that giving activates reward centres in the brain - literally proving that, as Jesus said, it's more blessed to give than to receive (Acts 20:35).

As dads, we have the opportunity to shape this attitude early. It starts with modelling: letting your kids see you giving generously - with your time, your talent, and your treasure. At church, to charity, in your family, to your neighbours, and those in need. Talk about why you give. Let your kids help when you donate clothes, volunteer your time, or give money to a cause. And when your child shares without being prompted, praise them: *"That was thoughtful of you to share your snack - good on you for being generous."* Ask them how they felt about it, helping them to reflect on the positive emotional payoff of generosity.

I remember watching the tragic coverage of the 2004 Boxing Day Tsunami with some of our kids. They asked me questions as I opened my laptop to arrange donations to the Red Cross and to support other initiatives in Thailand. This sparked an important discussion about how we can help in times of crisis.

Encourage your kids to give from their own savings or pocket money. This is easy with coins and cash: you can set up three jars for their pocket money: Spend, Save, and Give. Electronic banking makes this a little more complicated, but not impossible. The point is to teach your kids to manage their income and prioritize giving as part of financial planning. Encourage them to choose where to give - a special project at church, a local animal shelter, a food bank, or a cause they care about. The key is letting them own the decision.

The goal isn't to raise kids who just do generous things, but to raise kids who are generous people - kind, open, and willing to think beyond themselves. In a world where many people are selfish and stingy, and our culture is saturated with consumerism, growing up with a generous heart stands out like a light in the darkness. It's a powerful counter-cultural lesson to learn that happiness isn't found in hoarding, but in helping.

⚙ ENDNOTES

[1] Aknin, L. B., Hamlin, J. K., & Dunn, E. W. (2012). *Giving leads to happiness in young children.* PLOS ONE, 7(6), e39211. https://doi.org/10.1371/journal.pone.0039211

HEALTHY FOOD HABITS

My mother's menu consisted of two choices: take it or leave it.
- Buddy Hackett.

Teaching your children to eat well is one of the best things you can do for them. Kids develop their appetite and preferences based on what they're regularly exposed to, so if they grow up eating nutritious meals, they're far more likely to keep those habits into adulthood.

Let's face it - junk food is everywhere. It's cheap, convenient, and perfectly engineered to taste amazing, thanks to all the added sugar, salt, and fat.

And it's marketed directly to kids with bright colours, cartoon mascots, and catchy jingles. No wonder they're drawn to it. Studies have shown that high-sugar foods can activate the brain's reward system in ways similar to addictive substances. That doesn't mean your kid is doomed just because of a snack bar, but it does mean *you* need to guide the balance early on.

I'm not advocating going full food-police. Total bans often backfire. When something is completely off-limits, it can become even more desirable - just ask Adam and Eve. The goal isn't perfection, but consistent, balanced choices that train your child's taste buds and habits.

Here are a few food guidelines we used with our kids in the primary years that worked well:

- No snacks after 4pm - so they'll be hungry for dinner.
- Fruit first at morning or afternoon tea - then maybe a biscuit or something else.
- Veggies at every dinner.
- Try everything once - you can't say you don't like it until you've at least had a go.

Of course, we allowed for exceptions; eating out, on holidays, birthdays, take-away meals.

Supermarkets are designed to tempt kids with eye-level treats and checkout lollies. It's called the "pester power" effect - and it works. So, stay strong. Decide what you're buying and why, and don't let last-minute whinging or marketing pressure change your plans.

One easy win is to make your own snacks. Home-baked biscuits or muffins are healthier than packaged ones, with fewer preservatives and a lot less sugar. Plus, it gets your kids involved in the kitchen, which builds awareness and ownership of what goes into their food - as well as a great bonding activity. Ok - full disclosure - I have never done this - but Ruth did - and our kids enjoyed many homemade healthy snacks, so if you're better in the kitchen than I am (which won't be hard) then go for it.

A balanced diet of fruit, veg, meat, fish, nuts, legumes, chocolate, grains, and dairy contain all the nutrients your kids need. Don't bother spending money on multivitamins - whole foods do the job better (and yes, I know, chocolate isn't one of the main food groups - but it *should* be).

When your kids start school, healthy habits matter even more. The good news is most school canteens these days offer decent food options, so lunch money won't necessarily go straight to sugar highs. But the habits you've built at home will shape their choices.

Some tips for fussy eaters: don't panic if your kid treats vegetables as if they're poisonous. Their taste buds are still developing, and so is their sense of control. Give them some alternative nutritious options they can choose from, so mealtimes don't become battlegrounds. Make things fun - perhaps presenting veggies in different shapes, or getting everyone at the table to see how many different coloured foods they can eat. I remember as a kid not wanting to eat carrots, only for my mum to present me with something special; "Oh no, this isn't carrot - it's…. Cariola". I got sucked in and enjoyed my boiled carrots under their new name. Having your kids help in preparing the food can also help - even when they're little - if they've been peeling, chopping and cooking something they'll be more likely to look forward to eating it.

Learning to eat well is a lifelong journey so don't give up or let your kids settle into labels like 'I hate veggies' or 'I only eat white foods.'

Kids will do what you do - more than what you say. They notice what you consume; if you make beer seem like the most enticing thing at the end of the day, how do you expect your teenager to turn down alcohol at parties? Have a think about your eating and exercise habits and consider how that affects your kids. You don't need to give up sugar, or become a gym-junkie, but we can all find a way to eat well, keep moving and stay fit for life. It's a great example for the next gen, and you get to enjoy the energy and feeling of fitness.

Ultimately, we want to raise kids who listen to their *whole* body, not just their sweet tooth. Teach them to notice how good it feels to be strong, energised, and healthy - not bloated, sluggish, or cranky from too much junk. If they get that early on, then when they're adults and there's no one policing the pantry, they'll know how to look after themselves.

As the saying goes: *"First we make our habits, then our habits make us."* Food is no exception.

★ USE THE MASTERY PRINCIPLE ★

If a book about failures doesn't sell, is it a success?
- Jerry Seinfeld

Anyone who's worked their way through a university degree or other tertiary studies knows you come across a fair bit of information that isn't exactly essential for your future profession. But then there are little gems that stick with you that really are helpful. In my teacher training, one of these was the *"Mastery Principle"*, which simply says: success builds motivation.

When kids experience success - when they master something - they're more likely to keep doing it, enjoy it, and get even better at it. That cycle builds confidence, self-belief, and a solid sense of identity. On the flip side, repeated failure leads to frustration, avoidance, and a sense of *"I'm just no good at this."* This is why the sporty kids tend to keep kicking balls, and the musical kids continue on with learning an instrument. They're good at it, they enjoy it, so they want to keep going. It feeds itself.

But here's the powerful bit: mastery isn't just about developing your strengths - it's also a great strategy for helping children grow in their weaker areas too. So instead of setting your kid a big, overwhelming task, break it down into small, winnable steps. Start where they can succeed - even just a little - and build up from there. For example, if your child struggles with reading, don't push them to get into a long chapter book that makes them feel lost. Instead, start with simple picture books. You can read most of the story and let them just tackle one or two words. Then a sentence. Then a page. Every time they get through a little more, they've tasted success, and are more likely to continue, with a sense of enjoyment and achievement. A child who thinks *"I can't do maths"* can grow to think *"Actually, I'm getting the hang of this"* if the learning comes in bite-sized, supported steps.

Psychologist Albert Bandura, who coined the term self-efficacy, put it this way: "People's beliefs about their abilities have a profound effect on those abilities."[1] Your job as a dad is to help shape those beliefs by giving your kids real, do-able opportunities to succeed - then cheering them on when they do.

Of course, every kid has strengths, and we absolutely want to encourage them in those. That's how they grow in confidence and find their lane in life. If your daughter loves drawing or your son loves music, make space for that and celebrate it. Feed their strengths. But don't give up on the weak spots either.

The key is to create a pattern of progress - small wins that lead to bigger ones. You don't need to turn your kid into a genius or a sports star - just help them have a go, get a win, and grow in confidence - the kind that motivates them and strengthens them to keep going even when things get tough. In the future, they'll be confident enough to give anything a go.

⚙ ENDNOTES

[1]   Bandura, A. (1997). *Self-Efficacy: The Exercise of Control.* W. H. Freeman and Company.

NAVIGATING FRIENDSHIPS

The only way to have a friend is to be one.
- Ralph Waldo Emerson

Friendships are one of the great joys of childhood - and sometimes one of the hardest parts too. For primary-aged kids, friendships can be intense, emotional, and changeable. One week someone's your child's best mate, the next they're not speaking. That's all part of growing up, learning social skills, and discovering who they are.

We found it helpful to steer our kids away from the whole "best friend" label. Sure, it sounds cute - but it can put a lot of pressure on one relationship, while leaving others feeling left out. Instead, we encouraged the idea of being a friend to many. As the saying goes, *some friends are for a season, some for a reason, and a few might last a lifetime* - but you don't know which is which until later. I've got a few close mates I met in 2nd grade at school - that's 50-plus years of friendship (which makes us feel ancient when we think about it). We've got so much history, we can pick up exactly where we left whenever we meet. These guys have seen me with long luscious blonde hair in my barefoot pseudo hippie phase, to being young dads together and now as mature (read older) men and grandparents (with much less hair and wearing sensible shoes). It's great having blokes who know you so well and who've got your back no matter what. Teaching your kids to cast their friendship-net wide early on gives them a much better chance of finding those rare, lifelong mates.

Schoolyard life isn't always easy. Your child might face teasing, exclusion, or even bullying. Some of these situations require real intervention, so obviously you talk to the teacher or principal if something serious is going on. But not every squabble needs an adult to jump in. Part of helping your child mature is teaching them how to handle conflict with kindness, courage, and resilience. Talk things through with them, give them perspective, and guide them toward forgiveness and letting things go. If we always step in to solve things, kids don't learn how to navigate tricky social moments on their own. So, use wisdom - sometimes they need backup, and sometimes they just need a listening ear.

One great value to pass on is looking out for the *kids on the fringe*. It's easy to chase after the cool crowd - but it's far more rewarding to show kindness to someone who's often left out. Who knows how things will turn out? I doubt Bill Gates or Warren Buffett were the most popular kids at school, or captains of their footy teams, but I'm guessing their old mates haven't done too badly out of those friendships. Of course, I'm not saying your eight-year-old should start networking for future gain - but teaching your child to be kind and inclusive helps develop empathy and gives them the quiet confidence that comes from knowing they've made someone else feel seen and valued.

So what helps kids build and keep healthy friendships? A few simple but powerful things:

- **Kindness and inclusion** - encourage your child to invite others in, not shut them out.

- **Good communication** - teach them to listen, to say sorry, and to speak up respectfully.
- **Flexibility** - friendships change. Teach your kids to adapt without panic or bitterness.
- **Self-respect** - help them know their own worth, so they're not desperate for approval.
- **Faithfulness** - build in your kids the strength to be reliable and trustworthy for others.

Friendships teach kids some of life's biggest lessons: how to share, stand up for themselves, apologise, forgive, and stick by someone when it's not easy. Helping your child *become* a good friend is one of the best ways to help them *find* good friends.

FOSTER CARE

There can be no keener revelation of a society's soul
than the way in which it treats its children.
- Nelson Mandela

Many years ago, I was visiting orphanages in Thailand, where I had once lived as a teacher and returned often to minister in churches and support other humanitarian work. It struck me that the kids in these institutions would be so much better off growing up in family homes. Suddenly, I had what I thought was a brilliant idea: *I'll tell all my Thai pastor friends to open their homes to these children.*

Now, God's never spoken to me in an audible voice, but in that moment it was like He gave me a loving slap across the back of the head and said, *"What about you?"* I realised this epiphany of mine wasn't an original idea at all - and it already had a name: foster care. People had been doing it for a long time... I'd just never thought of doing it myself.

Meanwhile, Ruth had been thinking about how we could best help the poor in our own society and had come to the conclusion that the most vulnerable were kids whose biological parents couldn't care for them. So, we did the training, and a year later two precious young brothers, aged 4 and 5, arrived to live with us. Leroy stayed for seven years and then was able to move in with his grandparents. Keighlan stuck it out right through to adulthood, and he's now happily married and going great.

Foster care kept us on our toes. Suddenly we were back in the thick of it - school drop offs, early Saturday morning footy matches, kids' birthday parties - all the parenting stuff we thought we'd left behind as our other kids grew older. There were some challenging times, but there were also plenty of highlights; watching both boys conquer their fear of the surf, seeing them excel at sport (swimming included, eventually), and even climbing Australia's highest mountain (I hope that sounds impressive to overseas readers, but locals will know it's more of a stroll than a mountaineering feat). One of my favourite memories was saving to take them to Fiji, where they were met with booming "Bula!" greetings at the resort, rode horses along the beach, and visited a local village. There, they played with the other kids, encountered the culture, and even braved the unmistakable taste of kava.

All this to say: consider foster care. There's a huge need for good homes to care for kids when their natural families can't. And there's more than one way to be involved:

- Respite care: This gives regular carers a break - either occasionally or on a set schedule, like one weekend a month. It's less commitment than full-time care but still makes a big difference. You're giving kids another positive role model and giving carers much-needed breathing space.
- Emergency care: Sometimes you get a call to take in a child - even a baby - who needs somewhere safe *right now*, often just overnight or for a few days.

- Short-term placement: A few weeks or months while a longer-term plan is worked out.
- Long-term or permanent placement: offering stability for the long haul.

You've probably heard stories about how hard it is - and yes, it can be. Kids don't always respond the way you hope, and there definitely are challenges. But it can also be hugely rewarding. It costs nothing to attend an information night and see if it could be right for your family.

For us, it worked best when our youngest biological child was in her early teens, and the two boys were younger. Our older four had already had plenty of care and attention through their formative years, so it was (slightly!) less disruptive. Personally, I wouldn't be keen to bring foster kids in at the same age - or older - than my existing children, but I know some families have made that work.

Foster care isn't for everyone. But if you are called to it, God will give you the grace for it. And from one dad to another - there's nothing quite like being part of giving a kid a home, a shot at stability, and the kind of love every child deserves.

Whether through foster care, adoption or a blended family situation, many of us will enjoy the unique experience of parenting someone who isn't your biological child. It comes with its own challenges, but also its own special joys. The connection isn't always automatic, nor is it guaranteed. It'll require more effort, more sensitivity, and more patience than raising your natural-born kids. But as you open your heart, and as they learn to trust you and know you, it can be particularly rewarding. Let me encourage all the dads navigating the glorious array of family structures and dynamics - it's not always easy, but it is well, well worth it.

SCHOOLING – WORKING WITH (NOT AGAINST) THE SYSTEM

The roots of education are bitter, but the fruit is sweet.
- Aristotle

As mentioned earlier, the main task of educating and preparing our children for the future rests with us as parents - not with the local school. Our kids are learning from us long before they set foot in a classroom, and even once they're in school, we still carry the ultimate responsibility for their development.

That said, schools are important. And most teachers are everyday heroes who manage dozens of personalities, subjects, and sniffly noses with remarkable patience and professionalism. They deal with demanding situations - and children (not yours of course!). They may even help discover a hidden talent in one of your kids. So, they deserve our respect, admiration and support.

The key is to work *with* the teachers and the school. To do so, avoid these common pitfalls:

1. Leaving it all to the school.

Keep on track with how your child is learning, especially with foundational skills like reading, writing and maths. Read the school reports, attend the interviews, and take an interest in the projects (especially if you end up doing it all yoursel…. I mean if you are *assisting slightly*).

2. Blaming the teachers for everything.

Not every bump in the road is the school's fault - or anyone's for that matter. Your kids will face challenges and setbacks - and that's ok. You'd be amazed at some of the notes and emails teachers receive from parents - from accusing them of ruining their child's future, to demanding apologies over a lost lunch order. Some teachers might not 'click' with your child's personality. Use it as an opportunity to teach adaptability, and how to get along with different kinds of people.

3. Catastrophising.

One rude comment in the playground doesn't mean your child is being bullied. Some parents freak out and even change schools over issues that could have been worked through. Life has its challenges and learning to face them - not run from them - will help your child grow and develop resilience.

4. Doing everything for your child.

Let them pack their own bag, talk to the teacher if they forgot something, and solve their own problems as much as possible. Children who are gradually given more responsibility will build confidence and independence (and save you bringing in their lunch if they forget it at university).

5. Only valuing academic achievement

Some kids love books and learning in the classroom - but not all. Others are brilliant with their hands, or have great emotional intelligence, or shine in sport or the arts. Don't measure your child by grades alone. The world needs more than academics - it needs tradies, creatives, carers, leaders - all kinds of people.

Also, think outside the educational box. Some of the most powerful learning experiences happen beyond school walls: family holidays, a day at the zoo or museum, even just helping in the garden or fixing the car. Don't be afraid to take your kids out of school now and then for a meaningful trip or experience - especially in primary years. A week away won't hamper their progress. And remember, time at school isn't just about *what* your kids learn, it's *how* they learn - to learn.

Home schooling is another option. Perhaps a little too radical for most, but we did it for a year. Well, when I say "we" I mean mainly Ruth - I'm the trained teacher in the family, but once we put together a curriculum and had it approved by The Department of Education, Ruth did most of the instruction and activities. It was a great time, but for us, a year was enough; we valued the local schools, the social interaction, group activities, and the time saved on prep. But I've met plenty of balanced, bright adults who were home-schooled all the way through - and both they and their parents loved the experience.

Remember, a quality school education isn't just about your kids getting top marks and preparing them for university. Our youngest, Keighlan, wasn't really into bookwork or classrooms. But he was a hard worker, practical, and good with his hands. A brilliant careers adviser helped us enrol him into a school-based apprenticeship in carpentry during Year 9 - just one day a week at first, then a day at trade school. A year later, he left school, went full-time with a local builder, and got his ticket before he turned 19. (oops, this could be the 3rd or 4th time I've said this #proudfatheragain).

The point is: as much as possible, education should be tailored around the child, not the other way around.

So, your child's schooling is a team effort. Support the teachers, stay engaged, and don't be afraid to ask questions - just don't be that annoying, nagging, parent who thinks their child is perfect and too precious to cope with some of life's ups and downs. Encourage learning in all its forms and help your kids find the subjects and environment that they're best suited to. Build in them an appreciation of learning, the value of curiosity, and the character to apply themselves when needed.

MONEY MATTERS

★ ★

I want my children to have all the things I couldn't
afford. Then I want to move in with them.
- Phyllis Diller

By the time kids are in primary school, they should be learning how to manage money. They'll be dealing with it for the rest of their lives, so the earlier they understand basic financial principles, the better. As mentioned earlier in the chapter *"Work is Good"*, chores around the home are a great way for your kids to earn and learn. They begin to appreciate the value of things when they work for them.

At this age, they should be growing in at least five basic money habits: earning, giving, saving, spending, and investing. These aren't just financial skills - they're disciplines for life that will shape your kids' character and set them up well for the future.

When our kids began primary school, we opened savings accounts for them at the bank, but we also ran a basic transaction account at the Bank of Mum and Dad. It was just a notebook where we tracked deposits from pocket money and chores, and withdrawals for when they wanted to spend some of their own money at the shops or on an outing. It was an easy way to teach simple money management.

In terms of investing though, we could have gone further. As mentioned earlier, we helped our kids save for their first car, and we also used an investment bond to assist with university fees. Our arrangement with our kids was that we would pay for half their degree (unless the army was covering the cost – thank you Hudson for enlisting) - the other half they could either use HECS (Government fee subsidy and loan program) or pay upfront and receive a small discount. But with the benefit of hindsight, we should have invested on their behalf in the share market. Interest rates for bank savings accounts barely keep in touch with inflation, but the average stock market return over the last 20 years is more than 8% - in Australia, and globally. Parents can buy shares directly or invest in unit trusts on behalf of their kids, with ownership transferred to them when they're adults. This can help save for house deposits and other big-ticket items in the future. Small regular contributions are an affordable way of building up a sizable asset. A recent comparison I came across predicted that an average bank savings account would grow a $10,000 deposit to only $18,000 over 30 years, but the same amount invested in the share market might net over $100,000. In recent years, more people are becoming more financially literate when it comes to investing in the share market, and there are a growing number of child-friendly investment vehicles to cater for these savvy parents. So, do some research.

Having said that, managing money for primary-aged kids isn't just about getting more of it. This is also the time to build healthy attitudes towards finances, material possessions and provision in life. At least 7 values are worth reinforcing:

1. **Awareness of materialism**. Teach them, as Jesus said, that "Life does not consist in the abundance of possessions" (Luke 12:15). Help your kids appreciate that the most important things are those

that money can't buy: love, faith, relationships, purpose, grace, forgiveness, laughter, family, and cereal (ok, you need money for cereal, but not much).

2. **Confidence that there'll always be enough**. In our family, we've always insisted on never using the phrase "*we can't afford it*" because it projects a mindset of lack or poverty. Instead, we say things like "*it's not a priority right now*" or "*we're in savings mode*". It might sound like semantics, but words shape beliefs. Just because something's not within reach today doesn't mean it won't be tomorrow - whether that's buying acreage for a family farm, or a kid saving for their own surfboard.

3. **Generosity**. We covered this earlier in the chapter on giving. This is a value you should be modelling, not just expecting from your kids. Make sure giving is a normal part of your household, not a rare occurrence.

4. **The value of saving and investing**. Teach your kids to delay gratification. Waiting, planning, and saving for something makes it far more meaningful and rewarding when they finally get it.

5. **Avoiding debt**. This one is more caught than taught - if you live beyond your means, your kids will likely do the same. Teach them - by doing it yourself - not to buy things they can't afford and then spend years paying it off.

6. **Contentment**. One of the greatest financial lessons isn't about how to get more - but how to be happy with what you already have. Help your kids learn to enjoy where they're at, with whatever they've got. Gratitude enriches the soul, kills comparison, and overcomes jealousy. And if you want to get even more philosophical with your kids, throw this line from Socrates at them: "He who

is not content with what he has, would not be content with what he would like to have".

7. **Stewardship.** Teach them that no one really *owns* everything, except God - we just *manage* what we've been given for as long as we have it. Whether it's five dollars or five hundred, encourage them to ask: *How can I use this wisely? What's the best purpose for it?*

If your kids learn to handle money wisely now, they're far more likely to make smart financial choices later. Shape their attitudes as well as their habits, because character will always be worth more than cash. Model good financial sense yourself, and give them regular opportunities to earn, save, give, and decide. Do it well, and they'll grow up with both perspective and prosperity - and be far less likely to ask for pocket money when they're adults.

★ EXPANDING THE BOUNDARIES ★

*Freedom is not worth having if it does not include
the freedom to make mistakes.*
- Mahatma Gandhi

I t can be tricky to get the balance right when your kids start craving more independence, especially as they move toward their teen years. You want to give them room to grow while still keeping them safe. Some parents have no idea of where their 10-year-old is, while others will hardly allow their pre-teen outside the house. I once knew a teenage boy who was embarrassed that his overprotective father still wouldn't let him ride a bike around the neighbourhood with his mates. On the other hand, I taught in one school where kids were roaming sketchy inner-city streets after dark while their parents drank at the pub. Both extremes miss the mark.

The key is intentional, gradual expansion - knowing your kids, trusting them in stages, and communicating clearly every step of the way. Here are some principles that can help:

Tune in to your individual kid.

Each child is different. One might be high-energy and eager to explore - wanting to visit friends across town or catch a train into the city long before you're comfortable. Another might be a homebody who needs encouragement just to go outside. There's no one-size-fits-all when it comes to boundaries. Be aware of your child's personality, temperament, and social maturity, and shape your approach accordingly. Developmental psychologist Dr. Michael Ungar says that kids need experiences that offer each of them just the right amount of risk, challenge, and complexity to help them grow.[1] What's too much freedom for one child might be perfectly appropriate for another.

Stretch their physical boundaries gradually.

Most primary school kids will want to visit friends on their own. But *"Hey Dad, I'm going to a mate's place"* just isn't enough information. Start by knowing who they want to see, and where they're going - ideally, you've met the parents and have a sense of the home environment. You might begin by dropping them off and picking them up. Then, as they prove responsible, allow them to walk, ride, or scoot to nearby destinations. Eventually, they'll be ready to catch a bus or train by themselves - again with clear expectations in place. Make sure you're always on the same page with your child. If they break the rules or overstep agreed boundaries, follow through with some consequences, rather than just letting it slide. This builds accountability and trust. When your kids honour the boundaries correctly, you can reward that with greater freedom - which teaches them that responsibility brings privileges.

Build confidence, not fear.

Let your kids know that *"the world is their oyster"* - not something to be scared of, but an amazing place to explore and enjoy. Yes, there are real dangers out there, but overwhelming your child with fear-based messaging can make them anxious and timid. Instead, give them practical tools and rules (like *"stay in groups"* or *"be home before dark"*), but keep the tone hopeful and optimistic. The goal is to raise kids who are alert to what's out there but not alarmed - confident without being complacent.

Let them make (some) decisions.

Instead of a long list of do's and don'ts, focus on teaching values and giving your kids space to apply them in real life. Whether it's choosing what to spend their pocket money on, navigating an awkward situation without adult help, or learning to break away from the wrong crowd, these moments help to form character. We're not just creating physical boundaries for our kids' safety, we're giving them moral scaffolding with which to build their own values and convictions. You can't be with them all the time, but they can carry with them the principles you've built in them for making good choices.

Keep the conversation going.

Boundaries aren't a one-time agreement. They need constant tweaking. Keep talking about what you agree on, what other families are doing, and how things might change. Listen to your child's point of view and be willing to adjust when they prove trustworthy.

Expanding boundaries isn't about cutting the cord and letting your kids loose - it's about lengthening it with care. You're slowly giving your child the tools and trust to handle themselves in the world - one decision at a time.

⚙ ENDNOTES

[1]   Ungar, M. (2019). *Change Your World: The Science of Resilience and the True Path to Success.* The Sutherland House.

HAVE "THE TALK"

Human development begins at fertilization.
- Encyclopedia Britannica

Bringing up sex and relationships with your kids can feel awkward - especially if no one ever did it well for you. But avoiding the conversation won't help your child. In fact, research shows that parent-child communication about sex is one of the strongest protective factors against risky sexual behaviour in adolescence. According to the American Academy of Pediatrics, kids who have open, honest conversations with parents about sex are more likely to delay sexual activity and make safer choices when they do become sexually active.[1]

The key is to begin early - before the internet or playground talk starts shaping their understanding. I read one expert in this area who said, "If you start talking about this when they're 10 years of age, you're too late." Your kids might be shy to ask you directly, but once they start having questions, they're old enough to hear some answers. However, with primary schoolers, you don't need to cover everything all at once.

Start with simple, age-appropriate conversations about how bodies work, where babies come from, and the importance of privacy, respect, and consent. Use correct names for body parts. Answer any questions honestly, but don't overload them with too much information. This doesn't have to be the talk that covers everything - just the beginning of a series of talks that will grow deeper over time.

Even if you feel as awkward as your kids to talk about this, be as calm and matter of fact as you can. If you're nervous or evasive, your child will pick up on it and might start to think the whole topic is shameful or taboo. Instead, aim to be the kind of dad who's open, safe, and ready to talk - you might say something like, "You know, there's stuff about how babies are made and how bodies change as you grow - I thought we should start talking about that a bit."

Don't leave the job to schools, screens, or peers. As a dad, you (and mum) are the most important influence in helping your child form a healthy understanding of sex, love, and relationships. They're watching how you treat their mum, how you talk about women, and whether your values match your words. That's part of the talk too - it's lived as much as it's spoken.

When our kids turned 9, we planned a special weekend away - father and son, mother and daughter. It was partly for fun and connection, but also a deliberate opportunity to step aside from everyday family life and start some honest, age-appropriate conversations in this area. Creating that kind of intentional space sends the message that this topic matters, and that your kids can always come to you with questions.

When to say what:

Ages 5–8 (Early Primary)
Keep it simple. Talk about private parts, body ownership, and safe touch. Let them know they can ask you anything. For example:

- "Your body is yours, and if someone touches you in a way that makes you feel uncomfortable, you can always tell Mum or Dad."
- "Boys and girls have different body parts. They're private, and we treat them with respect."

You can also introduce the basics of reproduction in an age-appropriate way:

- "Babies grow in a special part of a woman's body called the womb. It takes a mum and a dad to make a baby."

Ages 9–11 (Late Primary / pre-teen)

This is the time to talk more directly about puberty, changing bodies, and how babies are actually made - but still keep it age-appropriate. Talk about consent, emotions, and respectful relationships too. For example:

- "You're going to start noticing some changes soon - your body, your thoughts, and even how you feel around other people. That's totally normal."
- "Sex is something that's meant to happen in the context of love, respect, and commitment. It's not just physical - it's emotional too."

Also, don't just talk about biology - talk about values. Something like:

- "In our family, we believe that sex is something special, and just for a husband and wife. It's not just about your body, it's about your heart and mind too."

At the end of the day, this isn't just about giving your kids the facts, or delivering a TED Talk about human reproduction. It's about building trust and equipping them to make smart choices in the future. You want them to know they can come to you with anything, without fear or embarrassment. The more open and connected you are now, the more likely they'll turn to you later when the questions get bigger and the stakes get higher. So, take a deep breath, embrace the awkward, and start the conversation.

⚙ ENDNOTES

[1] Breuner, C. C., Mattson, G., & Committee on Adolescence, Committee on Psychosocial Aspects of Child and Family Health. (2016). *Sexuality Education for Children and Adolescents. Pediatrics*, 138(2), e20161348. https://doi.org/10.1542/peds.2016-1348

LET THE TEENS GO

★ ★

*The greatest gifts you can give your children are the roots of responsibility
and the wings of independence.*
- Denis Waitley

The relationship with your children changes as they grow up, and some parents struggle with this. As much as you love them and want to keep holding them close, as they grow into adults there is a sense where they move away from you.

Sometimes this can be dramatic; I've heard parents say things like; "My cute, cuddly, child went to bed one night and in the morning was replaced by a dark, distant teenager who wanted nothing to do with me". Even a milder version of this change can be hard to deal with. My first experience of this was when our eldest, Hudson, as an early teen, declined the offer to join us on a trip to the beach, only to announce later that day that he was going with some friends who had a lift organised. I was crushed: I thought, "We've lost him / he hates me / he's never coming back / where did I go wrong? etc etc". Ruth helpfully calmed me down so I wouldn't take it as a personal rejection - it was simply a boy growing up who wanted to exercise and explore his independence.

So here are a few keys to letting your teenagers gradually have more independence.

- **Start with trust - but keep communication open.**

Teenagers need to feel trusted, but that doesn't mean you stop checking in. Ask where they're going, who they're with, what time they'll be home. Not like a drill sergeant, but as a dad who cares. Make your presence felt in a way that says, "I care for you", not "I'm watching your every move."

- **Keep the door open - literally and figuratively.**

Teenagers need their space, but they also need to know you're nearby. Be available without being intrusive. Sit up for them when they're out late. Offer to drive them and their mates (it's amazing what you can learn from the front seat when they forget you're listening).

- **Pick your battles.**

Not everything is worth a fight. Haircuts, music tastes, fashion choices, and body piercings are not hills worth dying on, as they're - hopefully and usually - temporary. What's more important are character, values, and keeping loving communication channels open. If you try to micromanage all the details of your teen's lifestyle, you'll lose ground when you really need to address something important.

- **Set clear boundaries - and explain why.**

Teens still need limits, even if they won't admit it. Curfews, tech use, and expectations around safety are part of loving them well. Be willing to negotiate and broaden the boundaries as they show more responsibility, but don't lose them altogether.

- **Let them make some mistakes.**

It's tempting to overprotect, but growth often comes through trial and error. As long as they're not putting themselves or others in serious danger, a few bumps and bruises are part of learning how the world works. Be there to debrief afterwards - try to avoid "I told you so," and instead use, "What did you learn from that?"

- **Respect their growing need for privacy - but stay interested.**

It's normal for teens to share less with their parents. Don't panic if they're not telling you everything. Just keep showing up and hope for more than monosyllabic grunts in responses to your questions. Take an interest in their world - their music, their hobbies, their friends - even if it feels foreign to you. This is often more appreciated than you realise.

Letting go doesn't mean walking away. When your teens were little kids, they followed wherever you led them, but now they're learning how to tread their own path. So, at this stage, you're walking beside them as they take bigger steps into the future. Your role is shifting, but no less important.

KEEP THE TEENS CLOSE

Absence sharpens love, presence strengthens it.
- Thomas Fuller

ncrease their freedom, sure, but don't be so 'hands off' that you lose sight of what your teenagers are up to or who they're hanging out with. This can be a tricky dance. You want to give them increasing levels of independence, but you also want to help protect them from being unduly influenced by the wrong people or forces beyond your home and values. Teenagers still need boundaries - but they also need connection. The goal is to stay close without crowding them.

Communication, as always, is key. We found it helpful to continually re-negotiate the terms of agreed boundaries as the kids grew up. When they were little, every night was a family dinner - all of us sitting together, talking, sharing our favourite thing from the day, complementing the chef (invariably Ruth), and cleaning up together afterwards. But as teenagers began to spread their wings, they weren't always around at dinner time; youth group, footy training, part-time work, parties and other things filled their calendars. So, we locked in one night when nothing else was on - our "non-negotiable" family dinner. Most weeks we ended up with several others, but that one night gave us regular family connection amongst all the different commitments.

Some tips for staying close while your teens grow up:

- **Create regular connection points.**

Whether it's a weekly dinner, Saturday sport, or catching up on the drive home from soccer training. Build in small, predictable moments to check in. It doesn't have to be deep and meaningful every time - consistency matters more than intensity.

- **Show up for their stuff.**

Go to their games, watch their performances, ask how the science project went. Teens might sometimes act like they don't notice, or even care - but they do. Your presence in their world says, *I care about what matters to you.*

- **Ask, don't interrogate.**

Open-ended questions like, "What was the best part of your week?" or "What's been on your mind lately?" often go further than a rapid-fire quiz, and you're more likely to have a real conversation. Respect their privacy but stay gently curious.

- **Keep traditions alive - or start new ones.**

Simple, regular gatherings like games nights, camping trips, or extended family get-togethers help teens feel grounded. They may be spreading their wings, but it's nice to return home to a warm nest. It doesn't have to be fancy or expensive, because it's not about the activity, it's about the shared history and sense of belonging.

- **Watch for communication windows.**

Teenagers can be unpredictable. One day they're silent; the next they're up for a chat at 10:30pm. Be interruptible when it counts. Often the best conversations happen when you least expect them.

Research backs up what many parents instinctively know: connected families protect teens. A study by Harvard's Center on the Developing Child highlights that having at least one stable, committed relationship with a supportive adult is the single most important buffer against stress and risk during adolescence[1].

Teenagers may act like they don't need you, but deep down, they do. Keep pursuing connection, even if it feels a little one-sided. Don't get put off or offended if they're not as warm, cuddly or polite as they could be. Having said that, don't expect every teen to be dark and dreary - some don't disappear from view at all, they just stay closely connected with their parents right through to adulthood. If that's you, enjoy. If not, keep the bridge strong, so your teen can walk back over whenever they choose.

⚙ ENDNOTES

[1] National Scientific Council on the Developing Child. (2015). *Supportive Relationships and Active Skill-Building Strengthen the Foundations of Resilience: Working Paper No. 13.* Retrieved from https://developingchild.harvard.edu/wp-content/uploads/2015/05/Resilience_WorkingPaper_13.pdf

KEEP THE LOVE FLOWING AS THEY GROW UP

If we empty our hearts of self, God will fill them with His love.
- Charles Spurgeon

s we noted early, children have a kind of emotional tank that parents play a key role in filling with love. When kids are little, they're usually pretty open about what they need. They'll ask for hugs, cry when they're sad and respond directly to questions like "What's wrong?", "Do you want to talk?"

Teenagers, however, can be a little more... elusive. A classic parent-teen exchange often goes something like:

"Hi!" - *grunt*

"Are you ok?" - *grunt*

"You seem a little down - do you want to talk about it" - *grunt, exit stage left into bedroom.*

This is where parents need to develop some tightrope-walking skills to attempt the balancing act between giving your teen emotional space while still letting them know you're present, interested and available. It can be tempting to back off when the affection and openness don't flow like they used to - but don't shut things down. Keep the channels open, even if it feels one-sided. Your teenager may not say it, but they're still asking the same deep question they had as toddlers: "Do you love me?". Only now, they don't always have the words or willingness to express it.

So, we keep filling their tank - with words of encouragement, eye contact, a warm smile, and just being present without pushing. Love can still get through, even in silence.

Remember also that if you're not filling your teenager's emotional tank, someone or something else will - and the fuel they get elsewhere may not be as clean or healthy as what you pour in. I know a guy who mistakenly filled his motorbike up with diesel fuel, and of course the bike broke down 5kms later. But the worse part was the ridicule he suffered at the hands of his mates. In fact, the banter continues to this day. If you have a moment, please pray for him. I won't embarrass this boofhead by giving away his identity, but let's just say I know him wel…. ok it's me. *But the point is*, every human 'engine' needs the right fuel, and parents are the best source of high-octane love, security and encouragement for their teens to run well. If your teenager's communication skills are just on idle for a while, don't be put off - they'll eventually come roaring back to life.

"WELCOME!"

"Small cheer and great welcome makes a merry feast."
- William Shakespeare (*The Comedy of Errors,* Act 3, Sc. 1)

D o you remember as a kid avoiding certain friends' houses? The ones that were dark, messy or had a strange atmosphere - with parents who lurked silently in the background and never said hello or did anything to make you feel welcome?

And then there were other homes - bright, warm, and open, just like the people who lived in them. You'd be greeted with "Hi kids, come on in! Want a muffin? I just made some. How about a milkshake?". Then you'd wander into your mate's dad's workshop and instead of being told to nick off, he'd show you what he's working on, and even hand you a hammer to join in. Those parents knew your name, asked you questions and showed genuine interest in you. Some of these places felt like a second home, with the parents more like aunties and uncles than just neighbours.

I had a couple of places like this - in particular I had Mac Lindsay - what a legend. A high school teacher who became a Christian father figure for me - and for many other young blokes. The Lindsay home extended a warm welcome to all kinds of people. When I got my motorbike license I was always looking for an excuse for a ride, so I'd often join them for dinner - Jean was a famously good cook. Afterwards Mac would pull out a Bible, read a verse or two, and then in just a few minutes, unpack some insights that made sense and applied to everyday life. He'd then ask whoever was at the table about their day, what's going on in their life or any issues they were facing, and again, he'd take just a few minutes to pray for us. Simple, loving, and life-changing. Mac's still a great mentor for me, 40+ years later.

As dads, *we* can be like that. And our home can be that place - the welcoming one. This is powerful stuff, especially as kids grow into their teen years and beyond. They often feel awkward or uncertain in the world, caught between childhood and adulthood. A warm, hospitable home gives them a safe, relaxed space to be themselves and pick up a few valuable life-lessons.

There's a number of benefits when your kids - and their friends - feel comfortable hanging out at your place, including:

- helping your kid feel confident and relaxed about bringing friends home.
- getting to see who they're spending time with, up close.
- having the peace of mind that comes with knowing where they are - and that it's under your roof.

So, smile and greet them when they walk in. Offer them something to eat. Invite them into your workshop or garage. Make them feel welcome and enjoy giving the gift of hospitality.

ROMANCE CAN WAIT

All human wisdom is summed up in two words; wait and hope.
- Alexandre Dumas

As kids become teenagers, it's natural for them to start taking more than a passing interest in the opposite sex. Long gone are the days of "girl germs", and boys being dismissed as loud, messy creatures to be avoided at all costs. Now, hormones are happening, and it's only a matter of time before your teen feels a spark of attraction toward someone.

That's all part of growing up. But falling hard and fast into a romantic relationship too early comes with complications. Teenagers often haven't matured enough emotionally to handle the deeper levels of communication and commitment that healthy relationships require. And then there's sex. Physically they're capable. But emotionally and relationally? Not so much. Sex was never designed to be just a fun or casual act, but a deep, meaningful bond for a married couple.

If you've built a foundation of open communication with your teenager, you're in a better position to keep the conversation going. Don't just leave them to figure it all out through social media or friends. Revisit the talks you had when they were younger - only now with more depth. With our kids (can you still call them that at this stage?), we followed up our dad-and-son / mum-and-daughter "talk" trip at age nine with another version when they turned sixteen. The conversations may have been just as awkward, but the content was now much more relevant, and it reminded them that we were still here for them, even as they approached adulthood.

We found it helpful not to encourage the whole boyfriend / girlfriend thing. Of course, you can't (and shouldn't try to) control every move your teenager makes. But you can gently shape their view of relationships. Spending time in mixed-gender groups is much healthier than pairing off as lovebirds. We promoted the idea of having friends and not getting too serious with someone. I cringe when I hear parents talking up a crush or romance in their pre-teen, as if it's cute. It's not. It sends the wrong message, that 'yes this is appropriate for you at this stage of life'. Then when puberty hits, that message gets hit with hormonal fuel and things can quickly go to the next level.

It's much better to keep things low-key. Say something like, "Yes, all in good time, you'll meet someone right for you, you'll fall madly in love and get married - but for now you just enjoy friendships." Too idealistic? It can happen. Even as young adults there's no need to jump into the dating game. The right person will come along at just the right time - no hunting required.

In the most R-rated book of the Bible, *The Song of Solomon*, the daughters of Jerusalem are given this charge three times: "Do not stir up or awaken love until it pleases" (Song of Solomon 2:7; 3:5; 8:4, ESV). This is wise advice. Love should be allowed to 'rest' until it awakens on its own accord. There's a real danger in stirring up passions before their time; infatuation can be mistaken for true love, hearts can be broken, and even unplanned pregnancies can occur.

Societal pressures don't help here either. Teen culture often treats being in a relationship (and being sexually active) as a badge of success of identity. That's a lot for a young person to navigate and chart their own course through.

So, what can you do? As your teen grows more independent and gains more decision-making power, your role shifts from director to guide. You can still promote the values you believe in without being dogmatic or demanding. And you can be a sounding board - a calm, trusted presence when they want to talk things through.

Some teens may cruise through this stage with no interest in romance. Others may fall deep into a relationship. Most will be somewhere in between. The main thing isn't to try and control the outcome, but to be available with wisdom if (and hopefully when) they come asking.

DIRECTIONS NOT DIRECTIVES

The great business of parents is to fashion the souls
of their children, and not to force them.
- John Locke

As fathers, one of the most powerful gifts we can give our children is *guidance without control*, and that becomes especially important during their teenage years.

When they're younger, it's appropriate (and necessary) to lay down the law and teach them right from wrong. But as they grow up our job shifts, and we need to increase their freedom. Rather than telling them what they *must* do or who they *should* be, our role is to help their discovery of who they already are and guide their development from the sidelines. That includes their values, relationships, and the moral compass they'll use to navigate adult life.

This principle is particularly important when it comes to career advice. Good dads aren't controlling and pushy about what job their child should pursue - but they're not so hands-off that their kid drifts along without any guidance at all. Every child is wired with a unique blend of strengths, interests, and personality traits. Instead of steering your teen down a predetermined path in life, just ask thoughtful questions, expose them to a range of experiences, and encourage the areas where they naturally thrive.

Career conversations don't need to set anything in stone. They can just open doors of possibility. Think of them as ongoing, evolving dialogues rather than working to commit to a particular job path. The goal is to strike a healthy balance: on one hand, giving your child room to explore their gifts and interests; on the other, offering your wisdom and perspective as someone who's been round the block a few times.

A powerful example of this comes from the life of Sir Douglas Mawson, the renowned Antarctic explorer. As a young man, Mawson was fascinated with science and nature. Instead of insisting he pursue a career that was practical or prestigious, his parents encouraged his curiosity and allowed him to follow his interest in geology - even though it was an odd career path at the time. That freedom led him to become one of Australia's most celebrated adventurers and scientific figures, whose work helped shape our understanding of the polar regions.

Like Mawson's parents, we can be the kind of fathers who listen carefully, encourage curiosity, and help our kids connect the dots between their gifts and their future. In doing so, we equip them to step into careers - and lives - that truly reflect who they were made to be. You don't want to pressure your kid into becoming a lawyer when they'd rather be building a house. Some kids are born for the books and will love a career that requires a university degree; others are better with a welding torch, a camera or building their own business without any academic qualifications. The key is to find a career that suits the individual, not their parent's ego.

To help them think through their options for the future, ask questions like: "What are you drawn to?" or "Where do you feel most alive and capable?" Get them to try out work experience options that most schools offer. Discuss with them the features and value of different career paths, so they can begin to consider what looks right for them. Your role is not to dictate the outcome but to walk beside them with wisdom.

If your school leaver wants a gap year, that can be a great opportunity - but encourage them to not let it evolve into a gap *decade*. I've met too many young people who left school ten or more years ago and are still drifting around with dead-end jobs and no idea of what they want to do.

That said, it's worth remembering that career paths aren't as linear as they once were. Stats show that the average school leaver today might have 16-18 jobs across 5-7 different careers in their lifetime. Technology, workplace shifts, and entrepreneurial opportunities are changing everything. So don't panic if your kid doesn't lock onto their dream job or course of study straight out of school.

Teenagers often act confident and self-sufficient (and many are!) but keep an eye out for the ways your kids still need you. They may have big ideas about how they want their future to look, but they often require help with the execution and administrative side of things. This could be setting up bank accounts, doing their first tax return, enrolling in a course, or even just paying their car rego. I wish I had made a laminated card to explain the different insurance options and procedures to get your car registered - I could have just brought it out every couple of years and said, "read this" before having to walk through the whole process each time.

A friend of mine owned a cafe and one day a staff member came in with a bunch of forms she was trying to sort out. She was a teenager with a very chaotic family life. As he looked at the paperwork with her, he realised it wasn't for him as her employer to look at or sign - it was just general admin stuff she needed to figure out. This poor young girl simply didn't have another responsible adult who could help her make sense of it all. Don't let that be your kid.

At the same time, you don't want to end up enabling them, or have your kids treat you like their personal assistant; "here Dad, got the car rego again - I'll just leave it on your desk - thanks". There's a fine line you need to take between *helping* with the admin that life requires, while at the same time gradually *handing it over* for them to tackle it.

Give your teenager space to explore, but don't disappear into the background. Be the sounding board, the occasional reality check, and the guy who cheers them on. A father's advice, when offered with patience and humility, can be a guiding compass without becoming a steering wheel.

TEENAGE TORNADOES

The strongest of all warriors are these two - Time and Patience.
- Leo Tolstoy

A couple I know were jolted awake one night by a phone call from their young adult son who was living overseas. He told them his younger teenage sister was out partying at a pub. They assured him she was asleep in bed in their home. He persisted and said he had just seen her social media post about her under-age escapades. Sure enough, when they checked, they found her bedroom window wide open. She had slipped out - apparently not for the first time.

If you're raising teenagers, you may have faced moments like this. As much as we want to keep our kids safe, teens are desperate to spread their wings. Some will go to great lengths to explore the world and establish their identity - sometimes dabbling in alcohol, drugs, risky relationships, or anything that feels like "freedom." Others will cruise through their teen years without much drama, happy to grow gradually within healthy boundaries.

There's no one-size-fits-all formula. Another couple I know had no trouble with one of their teens, while another went deep into the drug scene. Things became so unsafe at home that the dad had to pay for alternative housing. He did all he could - supporting his child in court, helping them avoid a criminal record, and never letting the relationship go. Years later, that same young person entered rehab, got clean, went to university, excelled academically, and is now happily married with a thriving career. The parents' love didn't excuse the behaviour, but it was the constant that helped their kid eventually turn their life around.

That's the key: maintain your standards - and maintain your love at the same time. Don't water down the rules of your home just to avoid conflict, but don't withhold affection because your teen is difficult or goes off course. Whether your kid is a quiet achiever or a walking cyclone, your unconditional love will be the anchor they can come back to.

Teens will push boundaries in more than just behaviour - they might challenge your opinions, adopt new values, and develop tastes in music, fashion and friends that make you shake your head. That's normal. Respect their right to think differently. Listen before you lecture. Ask questions before you hand down verdicts. Conversations build bridges that rules alone can't.

Teenagers need both space and connection. Let them have privacy, but keep shared family times non-negotiable - meals together, civil greetings, and some regular activities. If they're spending too much time in their bedroom, they may be depressed or stressed. Gently check in. Let them know you're available and interested, even if they don't feel like talking. No matter how independent they may seem, teens still need their parents' support and understanding.

Remember; adolescence is an emotional rollercoaster. Hormones, brain development, peer pressure and identity crises can all hit at once. Aim for a balance that keeps relationships strong while giving them room to grow.

Some tips for handling wild or rebellious teens:

- Pick your battles. Save your energy for the big issues; safety, relationships, respect - not every haircut or music choice.
- Be consistent. Clear boundaries give security, even if they pretend to hate them.
- Know their world. Stay aware of their friends, online activity, and hangouts - not as a spy, but as a caring guide.
- Model calm under fire. In a heated moment, your emotional control will help more than words.
- Keep hope alive. Many "problem kids" grow into remarkable adults once they navigate their way through their turbulent teens.
- Maintain connection. Find simple fun ways that you can stay close, like a shared sport, activity, or just sitting down to watch a movie. Offer to drive them places - it's a low-pressure way to chat, and if you're taxi-ing their mates around, it also gives you a window into their social life.

Parenting teenagers isn't about eliminating all the chaos - it's about steering through it with patience, firmness, and a love they can't outrun.

★ JUST WHEN YOU THINK THE JOB'S OVER... ★

Give me a firm place to stand, and I will move the earth.
- Archimedes

When your child turns 18, they're officially an adult - at least on paper. They can vote, make their own legal decisions, move out, and chart their own course into the future. They can also make bad choices, forget to pay their rent, and crash their car. So, as the saying goes, "you never stop being a parent".

That doesn't mean solving all their problems or throwing cash their way every time finances get a bit tight. But neither does it mean kicking them out with no sense of backup. The challenge is to find the balance between *releasing* them and *supporting* them. Adult children need the space to make their own decisions, but they still benefit from your wisdom, experience, and occasionally, your safety net.

One framework I've heard sums it up well:

- Ages 0–5 → Caretaker (or "Commander" if you grew up with a military father)
- Ages 5–12 → Cop (or maybe "Co-operator" if you're triggered by the thought of Highway Patrol - you know who you are)
- Ages 13–18 → Coach
- Ages 18+ → Consultant

By the time your kids are adults, your role is to counsel, not control. Offer your pearls of wisdom - ideally when they ask for it. Unsolicited advice often bounces straight off and can even damage the relationship. That said, don't back away when you see a looming cliff ahead. A timely warning at the top is much better than picking up the pieces after a crash. Whether it's relationships, finances, or career choices, being a voice of reason can save them a lot of pain.

If your adult kids are still living at home, remember: it's your house, your rules. That means they pitch in with chores, respect your standards, and contribute like a member of the household - not lounge around like a guest. It's perfectly reasonable to set boundaries on things like language, alcohol, or where boyfriends or girlfriends sleep when they stay over.

These days, many young adults are staying at home longer due to the cost of housing. That's fine - unless it turns dysfunctional. I've seen 25-year-olds doing nothing all day while Mum and Dad still cook, clean, and fund their lifestyle. That's not love; that's enabling. Our approach was simple:

- If they were studying full-time → no board, and we even helped with uni fees.
- If they were working full-time → they paid board. Not a huge amount, but enough to prepare them for the real costs of living.

Some parents take it a step further - secretly saving the board payments, then handing it back when the young adult moves out, giving them a head start on a house deposit. That's a brilliant way to combine responsibility with generosity (I spent ours on motorbikes).

Notice we only had 2 categories to choose from when our adult kids were still at home; work or study. There may be reasons for a young adult not to be doing either for a little while, but not long term. There's plenty of work out there, as well as courses of study that can lead to satisfying careers - we insisted on one or the other, and so should you.

The bottom line is: raising adult kids is about stepping back without walking away. You give them freedom, you hold your boundaries, and you remain the steady place they can always come back to - whether they need advice, a meal, or just to know they're still loved. Whether they're 8, 18, or 38 - you're still Dad.

RELY ON THE ULTIMATE PARENT

Father to the fatherless, defender of widows,
this is God, whose dwelling is holy.
- Psalm 68: 5

've deliberately kept this book practical and non-preachy. If you're not a person of faith, these tips will still help you raise great kids. But I couldn't finish without giving you the greatest tip of all....

Invite Jesus Christ to be the Lord of your life.

You've probably heard of John 3:16 - the most famous verse in the Bible - for good reason, because it sums up God's love and plan for us all:

"For God so loved the world that he gave his one and only Son, that whoever believes in him shall not perish but have eternal life."

That eternal life doesn't start when you die - it begins the moment you believe in Jesus and surrender your life to Him. From that point on, you have access to God's love, grace, wisdom and strength to do life well - including being a dad. He's the perfect father, and through Jesus, each of us is invited to become His child.

Here's the truth: you can only do so much on your own - so why try? You're much better off walking by faith, learning from The Bible, and praying to God as you face all the regular challenges of parenting - and life in general.

For me, being part of the family of God - the community of faith, hope and love in the local church - has been a game changer. It's where I've found wisdom, encouragement, and friendships that last a lifetime.

So, dad-to-dad, I encourage you; check out a church, open a Bible and consider the claims of Christ for yourself. The best parenting decision you could ever make might just be the one that changes *your* life first.

All God's best for you dad-adventuring.

. . . .

REFERENCES

Aknin, L. B., Hamlin, J. K., & Dunn, E. W. (2012). Giving leads to happiness in young children. *PLOS ONE, 7*(6), e39211. https://doi.org/10.1371/journal.pone.0039211

Australian Bureau of Statistics. (2023). Schools, *Australia, 2022.* Canberra: ABS. Retrieved from https://www.abs.gov.au/statistics/people/education/schools/latest-release

Australian Institute of Family Studies. (2021). *Adolescents combining school and part-time employment.* Growing Up in Australia Snapshot Series – Issue 6. Retrieved from https://aifs.gov.au/growing-australia/research/research-snapshots/adolescents-combining-school-and-part-time-employment

Bandura, A. (1997). *Self-Efficacy: The Exercise of Control.* W. H. Freeman and Company.

Be You. (n.d.). *Physical activity and mental health and wellbeing. https://beyou.edu.au/resources/fact-sheets/physical-activity-and-mental-health-and-wellbeing*

Breuner, C. C., Mattson, G., & Committee on Adolescence, Committee on Psychosocial Aspects of Child and Family Health. (2016). Sexuality Education for Children and Adolescents. *Pediatrics, 138*(2), e20161348. https://doi.org/10.1542/peds.2016-1348

Campbell, R. (1977). *How to Really Love Your Child.* Colorado Springs: David C. Cook.

Chapman, G. (1992). *The Five Love Languages*. Northfield Publishing.

Chapman, G., & Campbell, R. (1997). *The 5 Love Languages of Children: The Secret to Loving Children Effectively*. Chicago: Northfield Publishing.

Darling, N. (2025, May 15). Busted! Does punishment teach kids to lie? *GreatSchools.org*. Retrieved from https://www.greatschools.org/gk/parenting/social-emotional-learning/busted-lying-and-punishment

Dunst, C. J. (2022). Systematic Review and Meta-Analysis of the Relationships Between Family Social Support and Parenting Stress, Burden, Beliefs and Practices. *International Journal of Health and Psychology Research, 10*(3), 1–32.

eSafety Commissioner. (n.d.). *Parental controls | How to keep your child safe*. eSafety Commissioner. Retrieved 8 September 2025, from https://www.esafety.gov.au/parents/issues-and-advice/parental-controls

Franklin, J (2018) *Love Like You've Never Been Hurt*. Lake Mary, FL: Charisma House.

Gottman, J. M., & Fainsilber Katz, L. (1993). Patterns of Marital Conflict Predict Children's Internalizing and Externalizing Behaviors. *Developmental Psychology, 29*(6), 940–950.

Gottman, J. M., & DeClaire, J. (1997). *Raising an Emotionally Intelligent Child: The Heart of Parenting*. New York: Simon & Schuster.

Greene, R. (1998). *The Explosive Child*. Harper Collins.

Hartley-Brewer, E. (2004). *Raising a Self-Starter*. Cambridge, MA: Da Capo Press.

Houston, W. (2025, May 17). Your Brain Loves Deep Breathing, Science Explains Why. *Neuroscience News*.

Jentezen Franklin. (2018). *Love Like You've Never Been Hurt*. Lake Mary, FL: Charisma House.

Keirsey, D. (1978). *Please Understand Me: Character and Temperament Types*. Prometheus Nemesis Books.

Kelly, Y., Kelly, J., & Sacker, A. (2013). Changes in bedtime schedules and behavioral difficulties in 7-year-old children. Pediatrics, 132(5), e1184–e1193. https://doi.org/10.1542/peds.2013-1906

Lee, N., & Lee, S. (2009). *The Parenting Book*. Alpha International.

Merz, E. C., Rosen, M. L., Kaplan, A. R., Friedman, A., Lenker, C., & McLaughlin, K. A. (2023). Socioeconomic disparities in sleep duration are associated with cortical thickness in children. *Brain and Behavior, 13*(2), e2894. https://doi.org/10.1002/brb3.2894

National Scientific Council on the Developing Child. (2015). Supportive relationships and active skill-building strengthen the foundations of resilience: Working Paper No. 13. Retrieved from https://developingchild.harvard.edu/wp-content/uploads/2015/05/Resilience_WorkingPaper_13.pdf

NSW Health. (2018, November). Reading to babies and very young children. Sydney: NSW Government.

Palmano, P. (2005). *Yes, Please, Whatever!*. Harper Thorsons.

Pollmann Schult, M. (2014). Parenthood and Life Satisfaction: Why Don't Children Make People Happy? *Journal of Marriage and Family, 76*(2), 319–336.

Quality Care for Children. (2023). A Father's Presence in His Child's Life Can Be Transformative.

Ross, C. (1977). *How to Really Love Your Child*. Colorado Springs: David C. Cook.

Sanvictores, T., & Mendez, M. D. (2022). Types of Parenting Styles and Their Effects on Children. In *StatPearls*. Treasure Island, FL: StatPearls Publishing.

Siegel, D. J., & Bryson, T. P. (2012). *The Whole-Brain Child: 12 Revolutionary Strategies to Nurture Your Child's Developing Mind*. Bantam Publishers.

The Fathering Project. (2020). Why Fathering is Critical in a Child's Life.

Ungar, M. (2019). *Change Your World: The Science of Resilience and the True Path to Success*. The Sutherland House.